S0-ERT-753

LIBRARY
COLLEGE OF ST. SCHOLASTICA
DULUTH 11, MINN.

WITHDRAWN

THE MERRILL SPORTS SERIES

under the editorship of

Lewis A. Hess
The Ohio State University

CONDITIONING

Fundamentals

Edward C. Olson
The Ohio State University

CHARLES E. MERRILL PUBLISHING COMPANY
Columbus, Ohio
A Bell and Howell Company

GV
481
.O36
1968

Copyright © 1968 by *Charles E. Merrill Publishing Company*, Columbus, Ohio. All rights reserved. No part of this book may be reproduced, by mimeograph or any other means, without permission in writing from the publisher.

Library of Congress Catalog Card Number 68 1 9 5 3 9

69 70 71 72 / 10 9 8 7 6 5 4 3 2

Printed in the United States of America

Foreword

THE MERRILL SPORTS SERIES has been developed with two primary objectives in mind. First, to improve the teaching and learning of sports and secondly, to assist those who wish to develop or improve their knowledges, understandings, and competence in a variety of sports. These publications are in keeping with the modern educational trend, which places more responsibility on the individual for his learning, growth, and development. The development of a satisfactory proficiency in the area of sports involves a series of complex learning experiences. To use the best available learning processes it is essential that as many avenues of learning as possible be brought into play. This involves reading, listening, visualizing, observing, and actual participation. These texts take this into consideration so that the student has an opportunity to learn in depth and profit from learning cues developed by highly competent teachers.

This series will provide challenge and enjoyment in a variety of sports activities. Competence in a sport will be improved in terms of knowledges, appreciations, and performance. Likewise, the more experienced student will find the publications a source of information in developing a higher level of proficiency. In our society one cannot claim to be "educated" unless he possesses a level of knowledge and performance in a number of sports which can play an important role in the use of his leisure time and the maintenance of his general well-being.

An effort has been made through the presentation of well illustrated, explained, and logically arranged analysis of skills and highly effective methods of instruction to assist in the understanding of the nature of the activity, the skills of the activity, and the ability to evaluate personal progress or development with relation to the activity. Each volume is meant to be an addition to one's personal library as a lasting source of information. The material covered is of such depth that participation will be enhanced along with an appreciation of a variety of sports' activities so important in our present leisure-oriented society.

The authors are highly educated and thoroughly experienced teachers and performers. They have made an effort to present teaching and learning techniques specific to each sport which have been proven as optimum methods of acquiring skills, knowledges, and understandings involved in participation of the particular activity. The use of the series, coupled with professional instruction, will result in achieving a more self-satisfying educational experience which should not only speed up the learning process, but should improve one's enjoyment of leisure time.

Lewis A. Hess

Editor

Preface

This book is written for those individuals who have come to the conclusion that physical activity is one of the basic needs of the human organism.

The information gathered in these pages is applicable at any age and by either sex. The chapters have been arranged in a purposeful, perhaps even unique fashion. The reader who follows this progression should find himself engaged in an enjoyable and profitable learning experience. This is not to say that certain individuals may not find it more to their interests to utilize just certain parts of it, but it should be clear that it is written for the novice conditioner.

The introductory chapter is fairly standard: an attempt is made to fortify your belief in physical fitness by relating it to effective and enjoyable living. Also, the disadvantages of the sedentary life are discussed. The ways in which inactivity promotes disease, death, and personal disintegration are treated. No punches are pulled; this is serious business and you should realize it.

The second chapter acquaints you with a method of evaluating your present physical fitness. The most valid fitness tests, which also have the factor of easy administration without fancy equipment, are suggested.

The third chapter is an attempt to explain what will be happening to your body as it goes through a conditioning process. The physiology of running, weight-training, and other exercise approaches is presented. It is an attempt to educate you to the facts and the myths of exercise. For the person planning to exercise without professional guidance this third chapter is must-reading. For that matter, if you contemplate spending money on an instructor or a commercial health spa, this chapter might help you to evaluate their competency a little better.

Chapter Four helps you to get started on your program. The importance of the first few weeks in terms of loosening up the muscles and getting yourself slowly into the mood are the bases for this chapter.

Chapter Five gives the most widely accepted approaches to cardiovascular or general fitness. Internal Training and Circuit Training are treated in depth.

Chapter Six gives specific approaches and exercises for building muscle strength, power, endurance, and tone. Ideas about isometric and weight-training exercises form the core of this chapter.

The final chapter is an amalgamation of the information applied to specific goals. Ideas are presented for the obese person, the underweight individual, and the athlete.

The unique element involved in this arrangement of chapters is that the conditioner can and should work as he reads. After scanning the book once through it is suggested that you go to your workout area and begin with Chapter Two. After evaluating yourself you should be just tired enough to enjoy a break while reading Chapter Three. With full understanding of your needs and interests you can then proceed into Chapter Four, *The First Weeks of Conditioning*. The exercises can be alternated with the reading at this time.

Chapters Five and Six demand some pre-planning and do not lend themselves to exercise alternated with reading. However, it certainly would not be unwise to check through the book before and after each general workout period in the early weeks of conditioning. Once you have embarked on a running or weight-training program you will refer to the book only occasionally for new ideas.

Chapter Seven is for specific problems and can be integrated into the action at any time.

The point is that the book is planned with activity in mind. The hope is that it will get dog-eared, stepped-on, even torn from *use in a conditioning room*. It is not to be placed between two bookends; it would be placed best on top of the plates in your weight room.

Edward C. Olson

Contents

1 **Why Fitness is Important**, 1
2 **Determining Your Present Condition**, 5
3 **Ideas for Understanding Your Physical Structure**, 25
4 **Flexibility and Warm-up: The First Steps to Fitness**, 35
5 **Cardiovascular Fitness: Foundational Step**, 46
6 **Building Muscles**, 57
7 **Tying It All Together**, 102
   Glossary, 126
   Index, 131

1

Why Fitness Is Important

Many Americans were shocked when reports after World War II confirmed that nearly 50 percent of the draft-age men had to be rejected or given noncombat jobs because of physical inadequacies. In 1954 another report made Americans sit up and listen. It was a report by two respected doctors on the relative fitness of youths of the United States and other nations. American children had inferior scores on tests of strength and flexibility to such an extreme degree that these doctors questioned their simple functionability in everyday affairs. Many studies followed to check the validity of these conclusions. In almost all cases American children reflected their unconditional surrender to the world of inactivity.[1] Finally, as if to lay a cornerstone for the growing interest in physical fitness, recurring reports by medical authorities on the role of obesity and lack of exercise in diseases and premature deaths among the middle-aged have received much notice. Kraus and Raab summarized many of these findings. A brief part of their summary appears in Table 1.

TABLE 1

Comparison Between Physically Inactive
and Active Groups

	Inactive	Active
1. Death rates from coronary occlusions per 100,000 males (ages 35-64)	Professional men, business managers, clerks 141	Workers 107
2. Coronary heart disease of men over 45 (per 100,000)	Executives, judges, lawyers, physicians 250	Farmers, miners, laborers 44

3. Autopsies from 3800 non-coronary deaths (ages 45-70). Percent healed from myocardial infarction.	Light Workers 3.5	Heavy workers 1.2
4. Among 652 male cases of sudden death from coronary heart disease (age below 55).	Sedentary 112	Strenuous Activity 35

Hans Kraus and William Raab, *Hypokinetic Disease* (Springfield, Ill.: Charles C Thomas, Publisher, 1961) pp. 96-97.

The studies are numerous concerning the kinds of relationships shown in the above table. To understand even more clearly the correlation of death and obesity, ask a fat man about his life insurance rates. The insurance companies base their prices on the brutal story told by the statistics.

Thus, it is possible to see the manner in which an interest in physical fitness has grown. Evidence of the harm involved in being unfit touches every age-group, from youth to middle-age to the very old. That there is a connection between being unfit at sixty and being unfit at sixteen is a most obvious one. It usually follows that the "fat little boy" on the block becomes the obese middle-aged man struggling for breath and life with every day after forty. Therefore, the appeal of this book is to begin a conditioning program while still young with a sound heart and a body not plagued by the diseases and disabilities which are a part of old age. "Old age" is more physiological than chronological. It is relative to the condition of the organism. Many thirty-five-year-old men are "older" physically than some seventy-year-old men. An examination of the muscles, the tissues, the vessels, all parts of each organism, would show that the fit seventy-year-old has more "life" in his body than the dissipated younger one. Thus, if long life has any value, then fitness is important.

Statistics are not available to prove that longevity and exercise are direct correlates, but figures can prove indirectly a fairly strong relationship as shown in Table 1.

But these studies and statistics all have to do with the avoidance of death, disease, and discomfort, some rather negative factors; what about the benefits in terms of quality living, the "good life," as some people call it? Of course, the answer is not simple. Happiness does not necessarily mean the same thing to everyone. Some people enjoy discomfort, others actually get pleasure from a high state of tension, some just wish to be free of pain and worry, and a few are happy only after great personal achievement. However, in terms of some fairly objective evidence relating to emotional and physical states of being, it is clear that the physically fit person has a greater opportunity to enjoy the various life-experiences than the unfit.

In a study done at West Point, physical fitness was correlated with emotional stability. Comparing dismissals due to psychiatric disorders it was found that no cadet in the top 7 percent on physical fitness was discharged for psychiatric reasons, but of the lower 7 percent on physical fitness, 13 percent had psychiatric discharges.[2] In most studies about adolescents extremely high correlations have been found between high I.Q. and muscular fitness as well as between emotional stability and muscular fitness. Perhaps the most dramatic description of this relationship can be observed in the following statement:

> Many of the children who shun purposeful activity appear listless and disinterested on the playground; others run incessantly around. When expected to engage in physical activity, these children are likely to hide or pretend illness. They won't cooperate in games, become excited very easily, purposefully make fools of themselves, and complain about the slightest injury. Muscularly, most of them are greatly under par—they are flaccid or extremely tense and easily exhausted.[3]

In turning to the tangible physical differences between the fit and the unfit some studies have shown the importance of activity in relation to such a matter as digestion. Most doctors now deny any deleterious effect of exercise on digestion. In fact, they feel that moderate exercise benefits digestion by reducing nervous tension through a decrease in motility and gastric secretion.[4] The most obvious effect, of course, is the toning and tightening-up of the abdominal area due to exercise. The role of activity in promoting pleasurable sleep has been documented.[5] Mild exercise is especially helpful. It promotes a state of muscular relaxation most conducive to sleep. When combined with other constructive approaches to relaxation it can be a great source for releasing tensions.

The subjective sense of one's own value usually entails in part his physical appearance. A feeling that one "looks good" often leads to a better appearance. The reverse is also true. Studies about posture and attitude have substantiated this point to some extent:

> A person's inner self has a functional reciprocity to the world. Posture, for instance, is largely a matter of habit. If good, it contributes to the appearance and efficiency of the body; if bad, it spoils the appearance and makes the body inefficient. Good or bad, if a given posture is assumed often enough, a neuromuscular response is established which becomes typical of a person. A person's posture at rest and in motion often indicates the image which he has of himself and expresses the attitude with which he faces life.[6]

Finally it must be pointed out that the entire area of physical performance, coordination, and skill relate directly to the training of nerve patterns and the ultimate dispensing of efficient movement. The trained person performs better, tires less easily, and as a logical consequence, enjoys his leisure time activities more than the untrained and/or the unconditioned one. To become physically fit for a sport is usually best attained by a general conditioning program followed by extended participation in the sport. Once the fitness has been attained the skill comes easier and better; and more important, the individual can participate longer at a higher skill level.

In the ensuing chapters you will be introduced to exercise programs which should bring about the benefits mentioned in this chapter. And, if in the endeavor you are stimulated to a way of living that grasps positively at such ends, then this book is worth many times the effort it took to write it or will take to use it.

References

1. Hans Kraus and William Raab, *Hypokinetic Disease* (Springfield, Illinois: Charles C Thomas, Publisher, 1961) pp. 27-37.
2. *Ibid.*, p. 150.
3. *Ibid.*, p. 148.
4. E. C. Davis, G. A. Logan, and W. C. McKinney, *Biophysical Values of Muscular Activity* (Dubuque, Iowa: Wm. C. Brown Company, 1965) p. 36.
5. Justus J. Schifferes, *Essentials of Healthier Living* (New York: John Wiley and Sons, Inc., 1963) p. 60.
6. L. E. Morehouse and A. T. Miller, *Physiology of Exercise* (St. Louis: The C. V. Mosby Company, 1959) p. 50.

2

Determining Your Present Condition

Before beginning any exercise program the conditioner should have a thorough medical examination. It has been said that vigorous exercise cannot harm the organically sound heart, which is true of the other vital organs of the body as well. It is also true, of course, that certain physical defects demand either a moderating or a cessation of exercise. In many cases, though, exercise is recommended by the doctor as an important part of the disabled person's therapy. The ideas in this book on the evaluation of self and the planning of exercise programs are made on the assumption that every reader has taken a complete health examination and has been diagnosed to be free of any organic disabilities or diseases.

The next step is to help you understand your "positive" physical status at the present time. In other words, the question now is not whether or not you are ill, but to what degree are you healthy? Since the ensuing chapters will suggest exercise programs in four basic areas, tests are proposed to help evaluate each one. The four basic areas are:

1. Cardiovascular-respiratory
2. Flexibility
3. Local-muscle-endurance
4. Local-muscle-strength

1. Cardiovascular-Respiratory

The cardiovascular system refers to the primary circulatory mechanism of the body: the heart, the blood vessels, and the blood. The cardio-respiratory system denotes the dynamic interrelationships between the heart and the breathing components of the body. If these systems are operating at only a very minimal level certain problems occur. The intake and efficient distribution of oxygen is poor, the heart beats very rapidly to keep up with even the least of physical stresses, and the blood tends to pool in the extremities of the body, thereby depriving the heart of blood to pump to the tissues. Thus, the conditioning of the cardiovascular-respiratory systems is the most important and the most fundamental step to all conditioning.

In the laboratory the condition of these systems can be measured by some rather sophisticated means unavailable to the average man, or the average physical education class. The best single test available that also meets the practical limitations is the Harvard Step Test, the validity of which is accepted by most researchers. As Carlston noted, "such large muscle groups are at work that the performance is limited more by circulatory and respiratory embarrassment than by technique of movements and fatigue of the muscles."[1] The usefulness of the Harvard Step Test in the non-laboratory situation is reflected by Mathew's comment that it aids in "classifying differences in fitness levels of young men into three groups: least fit, fit, and most fit."[2] The name of the test is a result of its original use during World War II on Harvard undergraduates. The Harvard athletes scored consistently lower heart rates than did the non-athletes; moreover, the heart rates got lower and lower with increased training (indicating better and better fitness), but higher when training ceased.[3]

Karpovich discovered that a Rapid Form of the test was superior to the original test (Long Form). He found it just as reliable and it took less time.[4] This Rapid Form is recommended. The directions are as follows:

> 1. Step up and down on a 20-inch bench at the rate of thirty complete steps per minute for as long as possible, not in excess of five minutes. Stepping up and down is done so that the lead foot may be alternated. The count is equal to hitting on the lead foot every second, once up on the bench, the next second on the floor.
> 2. Immediately after the test, be seated and relax for one-minute. From one-minute after cessation of exercise until one and one-half minutes after, count your pulse. (The best method is to use the index and second finger over either the carotid artery in the neck or the radial artery in the wrist. Do not use your thumb.)

"Normal scores" or averages do not necessarily mean much. Everyone is physically unique. To place all people on a graph and make any lasting conclusions from it would be a mistake. However, in assessing your status, a chart of what is normal can serve as one guide to the planning of your exercise program. Simply keep the limitations in mind by asking yourself such questions as these: does my basic physical structure lend itself to this? What was my emotional state at the time of taking the test? Was there a temporary physical drawback such as a virus or a previous night of poor rest? had I just eaten?; and, of course, did I follow instructions precisely?

In that light Table 2 (p. 8) should provide a service to the conditioner. These scores are for college-age men. The peak of cardiovascular-respiratory condition is considered to be in the mid to late-twenties. For other age-groups slightly higher heart rates could be expected. Men who have been on athletic teams for several years usually score lower heart rates due to the conditioning which they have had over an extended period of time.

When your heart can supply enough blood for strenuous exercise without having to contract at an extremely rapid rate, it usually indicates that your breathing is fuller, your use of oxygen is more efficient, your volume of blood pumped per beat is greater, your peripheral circulation is better, and many other physiological phenomena are operating closer to maximum potential. The value of the Step Test is that it gives indications of your weaknesses or strengths in these biological functions.

The resting pulse can also be an aid to evaluating these biological functions. Several researchers report that there is a strong correlation between low resting heart rates and low heart rates after extremely hard exercise, especially among athletes.[5] It would be wise to take your resting pulse rate at this time and then check it periodically over the months to note any changes. The best time to take it is before you ever get out of bed. This is called the basal rate. One-minute rates of between sixty and eighty are considered normal. The American Heart Association reports that 76-78 is the average basal rate for all men. The most important factor is the relative lowering of this rate over a period of time by the individual through regular exercise.

A second use of the resting pulse rate is to compare your standing rate prior to exercise to that recorded after exercise. Obtain a normal standing rate for one minute. Then run in place for fifteen seconds. Immediately count the pulse for five seconds and multiply by twelve to get the minute-rate. An increase of twenty-five beats on the minute-rate is considered average; an increase of forty beats usually indicates poor condition. Moreover, if by forty-five seconds after the exercise

TABLE 2

Scoring Table for HARVARD STEP TEST:
RAPID FORM

INSTRUCTIONS: (1) Find the appropriate line for duration of effort; (2) then find the appropriate column for the pulse count; (3) read off the score where the line and column intersect; and (4) interpret according to the scale given below.

Duration of Effort	\multicolumn{10}{c}{Heart Beats from 1 Minute to 1½ Minutes in Recovery}
	40–44	45–49	50–54	55–59	60–64	65–69	70–74	75–79	80–84	85–89	90–over
0' - 29"	5	5	5	5	5	5	5	5	5	5	5
0'30"-0'59"	20	15	15	15	15	10	10	10	10	10	10
1' 0"-1'29"	30	30	25	25	20	20	20	20	15	15	15
1'30"-1'59"	45	40	40	35	30	30	25	25	25	20	20
2' 0"-2'29"	60	50	45	45	40	35	35	30	30	30	25
2'30"-2'59"	70	65	60	55	50	45	40	40	35	35	35
3' 0"-3'29"	85	75	70	60	55	55	50	45	45	40	40
3'30"-3'59"	100	85	80	70	65	60	55	55	50	45	45
4' 0"-4'29"	110	100	90	80	75	70	65	60	55	55	50
4'30"-4'59"	125	110	100	90	85	75	70	65	60	60	55
5'	130	115	105	95	90	80	75	70	65	65	60

Below 50 = Poor general physical fitness.
50–80 = Average general physical fitness.
Above 80 = Good general physical fitness.

Karpovich, *Physiology of Muscular Activity*, 6th ed. (Philadelphia: W. B. Saunders Co., 1965) p. 241.

your pulse count is not close to the pre-exercise standing level, you may also consider yourself in poor cardiovascular-respiratory condition.[6] This little test is known as Foster's Test and is highly recommended for those who are not able to do the more strenuous Harvard Step Test.

Finally, it should be noted that pulse rates are affected by a number of factors ranging from heredity to emotional upset. For these and other reasons a test should be taken several times to be sure that it is a valid reflection of your condition. And, since a test like the Harvard Step Test is a conditioner in itself, such a suggestion serves a double purpose.

2. Flexibility

Flexibility, or the range of movement about a joint, is the next component of fitness which should be evaluated. Loosening-up exercises should be performed for several days before making any real test of your full ability on this or any of the other factors. Simply performing the tests, which will be suggested in this section, at less than full effort would be a wise approach.

FIGURE 1. *The Standing and Reaching Test*

Instructions:
 1. *Stand erect with hands at side, knees straight, feet together.*
 2. *Keeping the knees straight, lean down slowly and attempt to touch the floor with your fingertips. Hold for count of 3.*

The reason that pre-conditioning is so important lies in the importance of being flexible itself. A property stretches in proportion to its ability to return to its original shape. This is the limit which Hooke's Law places to some degree upon the properties of the body. It follows, therefore, that injuries can occur whenever this limit is broken by a sudden movement beyond the individual's capacity for extensibility (flexibility). By evaluating this limit early in a conditioning program you may be saved the grief of a painful and restricting injury. Since Hooke's Law does not hold strictly because of the structures within a muscle like blood vessels, connective tissue, and fat, a series of stretching exercises over a period of weeks can increase these limits.

The Kraus-Weber Tests measured both strength and flexibility. It was questioned whether the American children were weak or just somewhat inflexible. Perhaps the best single test of flexibility from the Kraus-Weber group was the one designated by them to measure "the length of the back and hamstring muscles." It is usually referred to as Standing and Reaching. See Figure 1 for instructions.

Other forms of this test are available which allow for a number score; however, the scientific measuring of differences on flexibility is not as important as it is on some of the other components. Therefore, the attainment of a functional level (in this case, to touch the floor) is satisfactory.

This is the only test suggested for flexibility. Other joint areas will be stretched as a natural part of the workout program, and there is little danger of injury even if they are below par. However, to garner some idea of what the range of motion for certain joints should be, Figure 2 is provided for you.

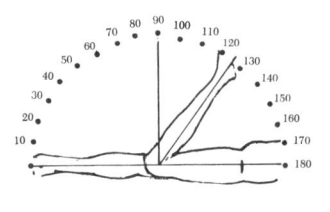

Knee
Flexion and Extension
0°–120-130°

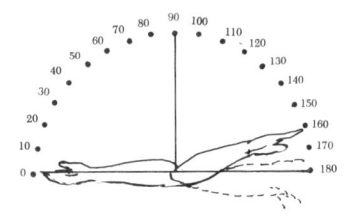

Elbow
Flexion and Extension
0°–145-160°

Determining Your Present Condition 11

*Hip
Straight Knee
0°–90°*

*Hip
Bent Knee
0°–115-125°*

*Hip
Extension
0°–10-15°*

*Hip
Abduction and
Adduction
0°–45°*

*Shoulder
Flexion and Extension
0°–180°*

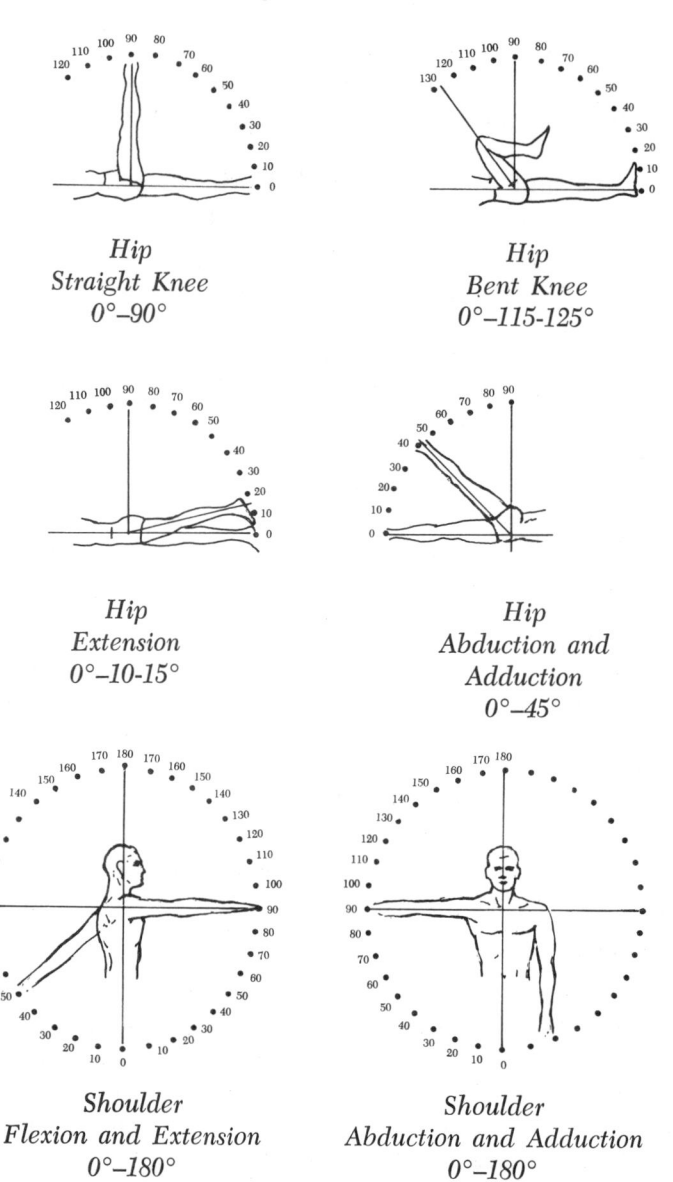

*Shoulder
Abduction and Adduction
0°–180°*

FIGURE 2. *Normal Range of Motion*

Reprinted by permission of Department of Physical Therapy, Institute of Physical Medicine and Rehabilitation, New York University Medical Center.

The value of these measures is that a less than normal score gives you a warning to begin your workouts slowly, something which might not be recognized solely through the tests which follow.

3 and 4. Local-Muscle-Endurance and Local-Muscle-Strength

These two components will be handled together in this evaluation chapter, because the tests which measure them are very often the same, especially where sophisticated equipment is not available.

Local muscle-endurance is the ability of a muscle to function at a moderate work load for a prolonged period of time. *Strength* is the ability of a muscle to exert force against a resistance. In most movement both factors are involved. The tests which follow make little distinction, but do serve the function of spotlighting some muscle areas which possibly need improvement in one or both factors. Again as with the flexibility test, several days of moderate practice on these tests is advised to avoid injury or a severe soreness.

A. PUSHUPS

This is one of the most easily administered tests for measuring the strength and endurance of the upper body. A low score on this test indicates a need for improvement in the following areas:

1. The triceps muscle (back of the arm)
2. The pectoralis muscles (the chest area)
3. The deltoid muscles (the shoulder muscles)
4. The muscles of the forearms.

See Figure 3.

Remember, on most of the tests to DO THEM UNTIL YOU MISS DO NOT QUIT. This means, for example, that you do not stop at the bottom of a pushup but rather on the way up. If you quit at the top, count it as one-half. The point is to give 100 percent, otherwise your score may be misleading. To work to this point of full effort will not be injurious as long as there is nothing organically wrong with you and you have worked up slowly to the maximum effort.

B. CHINUPS

This test is considered by research people to be the most valid test for measuring dynamic upper body strength. Used in com

Determining Your Present Condition

FIGURE 3. *Procedures in Pushup Test*

1. *Start lying on your stomach, hands directly beneath you, palms flat.*
2. *Push entire body except feet and hands off the floor at the same time. Come to a position in which your arms are straight.*
3. *Lower body by allowing the arms to flex an touch the chin to the floor. The arms should be at a 90° angle before starting the push up again. Count only ½ if this is not achieved. Also, count ½ if any part of the body other than the chin touches the floor.*
4. *Only four ½-counts are allowed. No rest is allowed between pushups. Continue until you can do no more legally.*

bination with the pushups (done on different days, of course) chinups can give an excellent evaluation of your upper body fitness. Chinups indicate possible weaknesses in the following areas:
1. The biceps brachii muscles (front of the arm)
2. Latissimus dorsi muscles (large muscles covering the back)
3. The gripping muscles of the hands and forearms.
4. The deltoid muscles (shoulders).

See Figure 4 (p. 14).

Again, and especially on chinups, miss as you struggle to get up. Do t quit just as you reach the bottom, try to get back up.

FIGURE 4. *Procedures in Chinup Test*

1. *After chalking both palms, leap to a hanging position from the bar with the arms fully extended. Your grip on the bar should be with the palms toward you. Your hands should be directly above your shoulders.*
2. *After a brief pause in the hanging position, pull yourself up with your arms and touch your chin above the bar. Do not kick your legs out, twist your body, or pull one arm at a time. Have a partner prevent any leg kicking by holding his arm in front of your legs. Count only ½ for chinups done in such manner.*
3. *Return to a full hanging position. Count this as one chinup. Continue until you can do no more legally. One-half counts should be made if you do not get your chin over the bar or do not come to a full hanging position. Only four ½-counts should be allowed.*

C. TWO-MINUTE BENT-KNEE SITUPS

This test measures the condition of the abdominal muscles as well as it is possible to do. The problem of eliminating the us

Determining Your Present Condition 15

of other muscles that help to flex the trunk is difficult, but by bending the knees it is possible to put most of the stress on the abdominal area.

Great caution is needed here to avoid severe soreness and disabling lower back pain. Follow directions very carefully. See Figure 5.

FIGURE 5. *Procedures in Situps Test*

1. *Lie on your back on the mat in a place where you can stabilize your feet. Bend your knees so that the legs are angled to the mat at about a 45° angle (the feet should almost be flat on the mat). Clasp your hands behind your neck with your shoulders flat on the mat.*
2. *Begin by raising your upper trunk to a point where your head is between your knees. This motion should start with your head and shoulders, NOT YOUR BACK. The back should be very rounded as you come up and the hands should remain clasped.*
3. *Lower to the mat just far enough to touch the points of your scapulae (shoulder blades). Count this as one. Continue for as much of the two minutes as possible. Count only ½ for any situp done without the hands being clasped, the knees being bent, or without full range of movement up and back. Resting is not allowed. The count stops at such a point. Only four ½-counts are allowed.*

A good steady pace usually is more successful than periodic sprints. Keep struggling even when it hurts until your muscles clearly fail to bring you up. Your abdomen will be quite sore after an all-out effort. This is not dangerous, but to reduce the severity, do moderate doses of situps for a week or so before any all-out test.

FIGURE 6. *Procedures in the Standing Broad Jump*

1. *Use a mat as the starting line. Stand on it with the feet several inches apart. Bend the knees and swing the arms.*
2. *Jump as far forward as possible by simultaneously extending the knees and swinging the arms forward.*
3. *If you do not fall backwards, measure the distance from your back heel to the edge of the mat.*

D. STANDING BROAD JUMP
This test has been shown to be the best single measure of leg power. Used in combination with the Step Test it should give you a good idea of the condition of your legs. See Figure 6 for directions.

Three jumps are sufficient usually to get a fair evaluation. Count the best of your three jumps.

The Normal Scores for tests A-D are listed in Table 3. Many other tests are available to give a more complete and more scientific evaluation of your physical condition, but these are the best ones available for the person or school without a great deal of equipment. Moreover, the suggestions in the chapters which follow are based upon an analysis and understanding of your scores in these particular tests.

The following approach to administering the six tests is suggested to help you in avoiding severe soreness and in obtaining valid scores:

FIRST DAY: No real testing
1. Perform some flexibility exercises slowly.
    a. Standing and bobbing (same as standing and reaching, only bob rather than hold). Do 5.
    b. Upper trunk twists—slowly. Do 3 to each side. See Figure 7 (p. 19).
    c. Side straddle hops (Jumping Jacks). Do 7. See Figure 8 (p. 19).
2. Do the FOSTER TEST.
3. Do the BENT-KNEE SITUPS test, but only for 30-seconds. Slowly.
4. Do the PUSHUPS test, but only about one-half of what you believe to be your maximum capacity.

Rest between each exercise at least until your breathing is close to normal.

SECOND DAY: (Two days later)
Do the same thing as the first day, but with slightly higher dosages. Add a few chinups this second day and do the activity of the Harvard Step test for about one-minute.

Continue every other day until you feel ready to try a maximum effort on the tests. At ages eighteen and nineteen, this is usually within four or five workout days or about ten days from starting.

TABLE 3

Normal Scores for Tests A-D

Percentile Score	Pushups	Chinups*	Situps	Standing Broad Jump*
99th	68.5	21	91	8'11"
95th	64.5	17	86.5	8'4"
90th	60.5	15	81.5	8'1"
85th	56.5	13	77	7'11"
80th	52.5	12	72.5	7'9"
75th	48.5	11	68	7'8"
70th	44.5	10	63	7'5"
65th	40.5	—	58.5	—
60th	36.5	9	54	7'3"
55th	32.5	—	49.5	—
50th	28	8.5	44.5	7'1"
45th	24	—	40	—
40th	20	8	35.5	6'11"
35th	16	7.5	31	—
30th	12	7	26	6'9"
25th	8	6	21.5	6'7"
20th	4	5	17	6'6"
15th	0	4	12.5	6'4"
10th	0	3	8	6'2"
5th	0	1	3	5'10"
2nd	0	0	0	5'4"

All scores were obtained on men within one year of their eighteenth birthday. Pushups and Situps scores were gathered by the author in conditioning classes at The Ohio State University.

---

* Chinups and Standing Broad Jump scores are reprinted from Edwin A. Fleishman's *Measurement of Physical Fitness*, 1964, pp. 114-116. Reprinted by permission of Prentice-Hall Inc., Englewood Cliffs, N. J.

FIFTH DAY: First testing day.
1. Warmup with about 10 side-straddle hops.
2. Do the STANDING AND REACHING test.
3. Rest about 30 seconds.
4. Do the STANDING BROAD JUMP test.

FIGURE 7.
Upper Trunk Twists

FIGURE 8.
Side-Straddle Hops

  5. Rest about 1 minute.
  6. Do the CHINUPS test.
  7. Rest about 5 minutes.
  8. Do the HARVARD STEP test.

SIXTH DAY: Second testing day.
  1. Warmup.
  2. STANDING AND REACHING test. Second score.
  3. Rest about 30 seconds.
  4. STANDING BROAD JUMP test. Second score.
  5. Rest about 1 minute.
  6. Do the PUSHUPS test.
  7. Rest about 8 minutes.
  8. Do the TWO-MINUTE BENT-KNEE SITUPS test.

This order can be followed individually or in a classroom situation. Those tests not taken a second time could be done on a third testing day. It is recommended that the order and rest interval be honored to keep the scores valid and reliable.

Somatotyping

This chapter would be incomplete if something were not said about the performance limitations that are imposed by one's body build. Perhaps the most overworked cliché is, "all people are not alike." Overworked or not, if this point is not considered, misunderstanding can occur. The term somatotype will be used hereafter to mean body build or physique. It is a better term because it indicates a classification of body types, a quantitative concept that lends itself to generalizations about physical strengths, weaknesses, and potentials.

Dr. William Sheldon devised the somatotyping system because he felt that "average scores" (norms) were meaningless when they ignored basic structural differences among people. For example, some people might never do twenty chinups, or lower their pulse rate below fifty per minute on the HARVARD STEP TEST, simply because they were born with a physical makeup incapable of doing so.

The somatotyping system is based on three basic body types: *endomorphs* (fat people), *mesomorphs* (muscular people), and *ectomorphs* (bony, stretched-out people). These parenthetical descriptions are not fully accurate, but in essence, they indicate what Sheldon means. A scale of seven is used to gauge the degree to which a person is one of the three types. A score of "7" indicates a maximal dominance of the characteristic and is seldom seen. Most people are composites of all three with tendencies toward one type of less than the extreme amount. The three scores for each component are given as in Figure 9 with endomorphy always first, mesomorphy second, and the estimate of ectomorphy third.

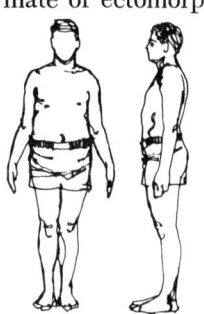

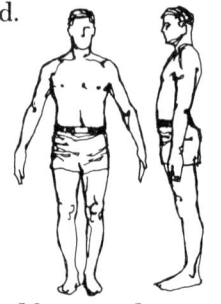

Endomorph-type
632 (Somatotype Score)

Mesomorph-type
271 (Somatotype Score)

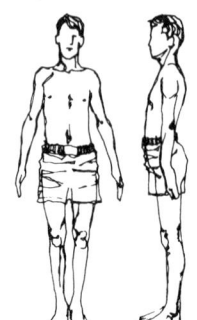

Ectomorph-type
136 (Somatotype Scor*

FIGURE 9. Sample Somatotypes

Cureton has developed a method by which the average person can somatotype himself. This method may be objectified and given more precision by having your physical education instructor or a friend also make a somatotype judgment. Cureton calls it the Physique Rating and it is reprinted here for you in Table 4.

TABLE 4

Physique Rating Scale

A. Scale for Rating Endomorphic Characteristics

1	2	3	4	5	6	7
Extremely low in adipose tissue and relatively small anterior-posterior dimensions of the lower trunk		Average tissue and physical build of lower trunk			Extremely obese with large quantities of adipose tissue and an unproportionately thick abdominal region	

B. Scale for Rating Muscular Development and Condition

1	2	3	4	5	6	7
Extremely underdeveloped and poorly conditioned muscles squeezed or pushed in the contracted states (Biceps, Abdominals, Thighs, Calves)		Average in skeletal muscular development and condition			Extremely developed with large and hard muscles in the contracted state, firm under forceful squeezing	

C. Scale for Rating Skeletal Development (Ectomorphic Component)

1	2	3	4	5	6	7
Extremely thick and heavy bones, short and ponderous skeleton with relatively great cross-section of ankle, knee and elbow joints		Average size bones and joints in cross-section and length			Extremely thin frail bones, tall linear skeleton with relatively small cross-section of ankle and elbow joints	

Cureton, *Physical Fitness Appraisal and Guidance* (St. Louis: The C. V. Mosby Co., 1947), p. 120.

Sheldon advises that ectomorphy is the most fixed component and the easiest to gauge; mesomorphy may fool the observer due to the effect of exercise; and, endomorphy will be the most difficult to judge because of the great effect that such things as nutrition, exercise, drugs, emotion, and elasticity of tissue have upon these types of people.[7] Moreover, he has noted that the year or two just before adolescence is the best indicator of what the somatotype will be over a lifetime. His evidence suggests that somatotype is constant throughout life (given normal nutrition and the absence of gross pathology), but that the "fooling years" are the adolescent ones, usually thirteen to seventeen. It is suggested, therefore, that you keep good weight records throughout your lifetime. For purposes of very accurate somatotyping the heaviest weight ever achieved by an individual is used. For details on the scientific measuring of somatotype as well as more information about the characteristics of each component you are referred to Sheldon's *Atlas of Men*.

Once you have discerned your somatotype, even loosely through the Physique Rating scale, you should be able to judge better your limitations and potential. The full meaning of this can be understood best in the context of your growth expectations. Therefore, in Chapter Seven where the subject of weight control is discussed, the somatotype value will be utilized further.

For immediate purposes the somatotype can prove useful in analyzing your scores on the fitness tests that you have just taken. Laboratory research has provided the following evidence relating somatotypes to fitness capacities and coordination abilities:

1. The linear types, especially mesomorphic ectomorphs (245 or 244), perform better than other types on baseball throw, standing broad jump, 50-yard dash, and 440-yard run.[8]
2. One research team grouped the somatotypes and found "norms" for college men on the following fitness tests:[9]
   A. Situps—Two minutes
      Moderate Mesomorphs
      Mesomorphs   } 46-50
      Ectomorphic Mesomorphs

      Mesomorphic Ectomorphs
      Moderate Ectomorphs   } 41-45
      Endomorphic Mesomorphs

Moderate Endomorphs Balanced Endomorph Mesomorphs Ectomorphs Mesomorphic Endomorphs	36-41
Endomorphs	33-35

B. Pullups (Chinups)

Ectomorphic Mesomorphs Mesomorphs Ectomorph Mesomorphs	9-11
Moderate Mesomorphs Endomorphic Mesomorphs Mesomorphic Ectomorphs	7-9
Ectomorphs Endomorph Mesomorphs Moderate Ectomorphs Balanced	4-6
Mesomorphic Endomorph Moderate Endomorph Endomorph	1-3

3. The following generalizations from a study by Sills and Everett summarize what many others also have found:
    A. Mesomorphs are stronger than endomorphs and ectomorphs.
    B. Endomorphs are stronger by a little than ectomorphs.
    C. Ectomorphs are superior to endomorphs in speed, agility, and endurance.
    D. Mesomorphs are superior to both endomorphs and ectomorphs in agility, speed, and endurance.
    E. Excess weight is a handicap to endomorphs and insufficient strength is a handicap to ectomorphs in the performance of physical tests.[10]

It would seem only sensible for both the conditioner and the physical education instructor to keep these "norms" in mind as well as those listed in Table 3. The mesomorph should expect more of himself on the tests, especially those in the strength component. The endomorph should realize that his first task is to reduce any excess fat, otherwise all of his efforts will be in vain. The ectomorph should understand his limitations for strength and his good potential for cardiovascular endurance. It would seem that this kind of self-analysis makes a great deal of sense in terms of individualizing the approach to fitness.

References

1. A. Carlsten and G. Grimby, *The Circulatory Response to Muscle Exercise in Man* (Springfield, Illinois: Charles C Thomas, Publisher, 1966) p. 53.
2. D. K. Mathews, *Measurement in Physical Education* (Philadelphia: W. B. Saunders Company, 1965) p. 201.
3. L. Brouha, *et. al.*, "Studies in Physical Efficiency of College Students," *Research Quarterly*, Vol. 15 (October, 1944) p. 224.
4. Karpovich, *Physiology of Muscular Activity*, pp. 241-242.
5. Carlsten, *The Circulatory Response to Muscle Exercise in Man*, p. 65.
6. Mathews, *Measurement in Physical Education*, p. 370.
7. William H. Sheldon, *Atlas of Men* (New York: Harper & Row, Publishers, 1954) p. 24.
8. T. K. Cureton, "Body Build as a Framework of References for Interpreting Physical Fitness and Athletic Performance," *Research Quarterly Supplement*, Vol. 12 (May, 1941) p. 301.
9. F. D. Sills and J. Mitchem, "Prediction of Performances on Physical Fitness Tests by Means of Somatotype Ratings," *Research Quarterly*, Vol. 28 (March, 1957) pp. 67-68.
10. F. D. Sills and P. W. Everett, "The Relationship of Extreme Somatotypes to Performance in Motor and Strength Tests," *Research Quarterly*, Vol. 24 (May, 1953) pp. 223-228.

3

Ideas for Understanding Your Physical Structure

Exercise programs have come a long way in the past few years. Trainers now understand in greater detail the way in which movement affects the human organism. This chapter will attempt to provide you with a portion of that knowledge. In a general cultural sense the people seem to have digressed somewhat in their appreciation of the values of movement. One need only look to the Greek culture of 450 B.C. to note the high regard in which exercise was held at one time. Some present-day reports indicate that modern man has allowed himself to forget the needs of his body much to the detriment of his total functioning.

However, some noteworthy steps are being taken to change these kinds of attitudes. In part the setting of world records in track, swimming, and weight-lifting help to bring about positive changes. They do it by creating an interest in the training methods used to produce championship performances. Interval Training has enabled many runners to break the four-minute barrier in the mile run; it has been utilized in swimming to produce performances once thought to be impossible. Weight-lifters have pushed up the limits of strength due primarily to new understandings in planning lifting programs.

What has happened in these and other sports has served to illuminate the fact that the human organism is amazingly functional. For the common man this is the important factor about world records. They indicate to him that his own body may be capable of greater achievement. The training programs used by record-holders indicate the approach that he might employ profitably.

Specific Concepts Around Which To Form A Conditioning Program

To outline goals for a program precisely is necessary in order to avoid wasting time and energy. If an exercise is done just to be doing something, there is some benefit (as in all movement if done correctly), but if a better exercise can be found for a particular purpose it would be foolish not to use it.

A general conditioning program emphasizes the development of four basic components from which other minor objectives may evolve:
1. Cardiovascular or generalized endurance
2. Flexibility
3. Local muscle endurance
4. Muscle strength

If these four interrelated objectives are achieved, such things as muscle tone, muscle power, and weight control are also improved. Some special exercises may be needed to bring these other components to optimal fitness, but in working toward the "Big Four" the conditioner will affect most fitness needs positively and effectively.

Cardiovascular Endurance

This is the most important factor of all. If a conditioner does not develop his heart, arteries, veins, capillaries, and venules to their fullest function he penalizes the development of every other fitness component. Gains which mark improvement in cardiovascular endurance were discussed briefly in the last chapter. In outline form these are the most important to keep in mind:

1. The heart muscle enlarges.
2. More blood is pumped per heart beat.
3. Fewer beats are required to do the same work load.
4. The arteries can handle more stress, are more elastic, have more capillaries extending to the body tissues.
5. Peripheral circulation is improved; blood returns to the heart quicker and easier.
6. The heart fills more during its rest periods.
7. The blood itself contains more red corpuscles, therefore has more hemoglobin for "grabbing" oxygen.
8. The waste products of metabolism are reduced and changed with greater effectiveness.

The respiratory system is also a beneficiary of a program to improve cardiovascular endurance. The muscles around the lungs become more flexible and stronger, especially the diaphragm which plays such a large role in breathing and "sucking" blood down into the heart. The diaphragm does not literally suck the blood, but by strong contractions it aids in reducing pressure in the chest cavity. This allows air to rush into the lungs and blood to reach the heart. Equally as important is that the lungs exhale carbon dioxide and other unwanted materials with greater efficiency.

Other processes of the body also benefit from an exercise program aimed at cardiovascular improvement. Among these are improved digestion and better elimination of liquid and solid wastes.

Flexibility

An evaluation of this was made in the last chapter with a warning that injuries can occur quite readily if the ligaments, tendons, or muscles are stretched beyond their capacity. However, the idea of being flexible has a functional purpose as well.

The matter of "better functioning" is not a simple phenomenon. The components of strength, endurance, the body-image, and flexibility are all interrelated in its promotion. It is very difficult to attribute an improved performance to any one of them. All seem to improve together and can disintegrate together. In terms of flexibility this kind of inter-dependency seems particularly true. Exercises designed to promote strength can very easily promote flexibility. To understand this phenomenon, one only needs to observe the ability of Olympic weight-lifters to do the exercise FULL-SQUATS. Figure 10 shows the weight-lifter's extreme extensibility in the tendons and muscles surrounding the knee. The average man usually cannot keep his heels flat on the floor and squat that low. Ironically enough, full-squats with a weight on the shoulders is *not* recommended for the average conditioner because his knees probably could not take the strain. HALF-SQUATS is highly recommended, though, and will be mentioned later. Thus, we see how flexibility, strength, and freedom from injury are interrelated.

What is really being conditioned by flexibility exercises is the range through which the limbs can move. This distance can be increased about a joint only so far. Various factors limit the range of motion, one being the joint capsule itself. Within the joint the fluids are affected by various phenomena to reduce the ease with which the bones move or slide. Cold temperatures, for example, tend to hinder flexibility more than do warm temperatures. More important, however, at this

FIGURE 10. *Full-Squat of a Weight-Lifter*

This kind of flexibility came from strength work

time to the planning of your exercise program, is the limitation imposed by the structures that surround and make up the muscles. These are such things as the fascial sheaths or outer layer of the muscle itself (the epimysium), the covering of the muscle fibers (the perimysium), and the tendons which connect the muscle to the bone. DeVries calculates these tissues to be responsible for more than one-half of the limitation involved in joint stiffness. Skin, the joint capsule, and the bone structure are the other limiting factors.[1] The softer tissues can be improved in their flexibility by proper stretching exercises; the hard structures like the bone cannot.

Two reactions can occur within the nervous system as a result of stretching a muscle. If the muscle and its tendon are stretched quickly or in a jerky fashion, a *simple stretch reflex* (myotatic reflex) takes place. If the stretching is slow and steady the *inverse stretch reflex* occurs. The simple stretch reflex is one of the most interesting evidences of the engineering masterpiece that is the body. When muscles flex a joint, extensor muscles on the opposite side of the joint are stretched. Via the nervous system an impulse reaches these extensors and causes them to either contract or relax. It is this difference that defines the two terms: a simple stretch reflex results in an *increase in tension* in the extensor muscles; an inverse stretch reflex results in an *inhibiting of tension* in the extensor muscles (or any muscles stretched by the action of an antagonistic set of muscles). It is this latter reaction that is desired in flexibility exercises. The inhibiting of the antagonist muscles promotes greater range of motion and prevents injury. For this reason it is highly recommended that all flexibility and most weight-training exercises be done slowly and steadily.

In Chapter Six the stretch reflex is discussed further in connection with improving muscular coordination. What is most important to recognize at this time is that the component flexibility is intricately bound to the idea of developing oneself in a balanced manner. The basic premise of this book is that the human organism is at its best to the extent that it is able to unify all of its attributes. Therefore, conditioning suggestions necessarily aim at the development of overall body strength and the promotion of a close symmetry of body parts. If one muscle area has strength far beyond other nearby muscle areas it is difficult for the individual to produce smooth, coordinated movements. In such a case the person may not be able to limit properly his flexibility and thereby overextends himself to the point of injury and/or functional ineffectiveness.

Local-Muscle-Endurance

This component is similar to cardiovascular endurance in that the main goal is to increase circulatory efficiency. Primarily, local-muscle-endurance exercises develop increased capillarization (more capillaries at work) in a specific muscle area. This additional aid to circulation in the area enables the muscle to ward off fatigue better. The differences between the two types of endurance, cardiovascular and local-muscle, relate to this complex matter of *fatigue*. Physiologists are slowly and haltingly attempting to explain what happens when a human "runs out of gas." The following explanation is derived from what is presently known about fatigue.

Muscles can be stimulated to contract by the nerve impulses coming from the motor nerve cells in the spinal cord. Many nerve cells supply impulses to a single muscle which is made up of thousands of fibers. One nerve cell in the spinal cord may supply 100-150 muscle fibers via a single lead-in nerve fiber which branches when it reaches the muscle. Once that nerve cell at the spinal cord fires its impulse, every muscle fiber supplied by its branches contracts. This is the All or None law.

If the exercise demands great strength *all* the nerve cells supplying a particular muscle may fire causing *all* the fibers within that muscle to contract, which seldom happens. In most exercises for local-muscle-endurance only a portion of the fibers in a muscle are contracted at any one time because the resistance encountered (for example lifting a barbell) is not heavy enough to require complete involvement. The value of using a moderate stress of this nature comes from the fact that the exercise can be continued for a longer period of time. A rhythm is established whereby different fibers trade off causing the contraction which promotes the adaptation within the muscle of certain mechanisms, an adaptation that would not occur in a quick maximal effort.

When the nerve impulse reaches the muscle fiber, energy is released through a series of chemical reactions. Two high-energy compounds, ATP (Adenosine tri-phosphate) and Creatine Phosphate, play the key roles:

1. The ATP splits to provide energy for the actual shortening of the muscle.
2. Part of the ATP is used during this breakdown to form other compounds, which will be used in the reproduction of more ATP.
3. The Creatine Phosphate splits to liberate energy to reproduce the ATP from these other compounds.
4. To rebuild Creatine Phosphate, food (primarily glycogen and fat) is oxidized. For example, the glycogen breaks down into glucose. If oxygen is present in adequate amounts, the glucose breaks down into carbon dioxide and water to be eliminated. Meanwhile, the breakdown or splitting of the glucose has helped to provide the energy for the re-creation of the Creatine Phosphate.
5. As a result of all this the basic products needed to start with step one are restored. The ATP may now act to help cause another contraction of the muscle fiber.

This explanation is, of course, an oversimplification. The adaptation process is extremely complex.

In normal activity or even very moderate exercise the body keeps up with this process without difficulty. The intake of oxygen and its distribution by the blood to the cells remains equal to the amount required for the rebuilding of the Creatine Phosphate. As a result there is no fatigue of enough consequence to prevent another contraction of the muscle.

When the activity is stepped up, however, it brings on the kind of fatigue associated with local-muscle-endurance. The supply of oxygen fails to keep pace with the accumulating metabolites (products of the energy-release) within the muscle. The primary metabolite that accumulates is *lactic acid*, a waste product which is normally resynthesized by the oxygen into glycogen, or oxidized into carbon dioxide and water and carried away by the blood. In strenuous work the oxygen supply cannot keep up with these functions and the lactic acid accumulates to such a degree that the necessary energy is diminished. The muscle ceases to contract, thus *fatigue* or *exhaustion* occur depending upon the degree of accumulation. The body must rest to allow the removal of the lactic acid.

However, with conditioning it is possible to aid the process by improving the efficiency with which it is accomplished. The key lies in the ability of the body to do two things: (1) Get oxygen to the muscles as fast as possible; and (2) transport the waste products away from the muscles as quickly as possible. The two actions work together. The first factor, better oxygen intake and distribution, can best be improved through special cardiovascular-respiratory exercise programs discussed in Chapter Five. The second factor is really basic local muscle endurance itself. By increasing the number of blood vessels (capillaries and venules) in a muscle it is possible to eliminate more quickly the waste products of muscle contraction. And, of course, the increased capillarization helps tremendously in the delivery of oxygen to the local muscle area.

It has been firmly established that more capillaries open up for use during exercise than during rest. Moreover, the conditioned man is able to increase the blood flow through these capillaries at a faster rate than the unconditioned man. If a man attempts to contract the muscle with an extremely heavy resistance, the blood flow is impaired; however, if he engages in light, rhythmical contractions with full movement many times, he is able to increase the blood flow through the muscles.[2] As a result, an all-around conditioning program includes exercises in which the weight or resistance is small, but the number of repetitions is high, the only way to develop local-muscle-endurance. A gain in the definition of the muscles is acquired as a secondary result, but one highly desired by many people. With extremely heavy resistance this factor is not usually improved.

This explanation of fatigue has been greatly simplified for purposes of this book. All the data have not been compiled on this extremely complex phenomenon. Some recent findings have indicated that the real source of fatigue is not within the muscle. It is currently being suggested that something restricts the passage of the nerve impulse prior to the time when it reaches the muscle. This blockage can occur either at the junction of the nerve fiber and the muscle, or at a junction (synapse) somewhere in the central nervous system.[3]

Be that as it may, one still feels sore *in* the muscles from exercise that is new or strenuous. This soreness usually dictates a slowing-down or cessation of exercise, which we attribute to "our fatigue." Therefore, any exercise program that can improve our ability to handle this "soreness" plays an important role in our handling of fatigue.

Muscle Strength

This component can be developed even if the exercise program includes only weight-training of the local-muscle-endurance type; i.e., light weights lifted many times in rhythmical fashion. However, it is well known that strength gains occur much faster and to a greater intensity through the use of heavier resistances lifted only a few times.

The reasons for this lie in the nature of the concept, *strength*. Strength is usually defined as the ability to apply tension in a single maximum contraction. It is not hard to picture the different functions in everyday life for which such a skill is needed, anything from helping the wife shift a chair to lifting the baby from the crib. The fact that one does not do these actions over and over indicates a need qualitatively different from that involved in local-muscle-endurance.

When a muscle is called upon to apply maximum tension, such as in pushing a piano or pressing a 200-pound barbell, it responds differently than for a lighter stress. More nerve impulses are fired from the spinal cord in an attempt to employ more muscle fibers in the contraction. It is thought that strong men are able to utilize more fibers when necessary than weaker men. To have such a skill requires the constant use over a period of years of fibers that normally would lie dormant, almost to the point of "drying-up." The average person never lifts anything heavy enough to require his nervous system to fully employ all the muscle fibers in a muscle area. He may do it once in a great while and strain himself because he has not slowly and progressively prepared his system for a maximal effort.

It should now be clear that a conditioning program must build *strength* differently than it does *local-muscle-endurance*. Exercises for

Ideas for Understanding Your Physical Structure

strength must involve heavier weights that can only be raised a few times and with great effort. Otherwise, certain muscle fibers will never be used.

All that happens to the strong man relative to the weaker man is not entirely clear, but the following points are considered valid at this time:

1. Strong men are able to employ their muscle fibers more fully to heavier work tasks.
2. Strong men develop more and better neural pathways to a muscle area making possible more effective employment of nerve impulses for greater muscular speed and coordination.
3. Usually the cross-section of the muscle fibers become larger in strong men.
4. The strong man's muscle fibers realign themselves to improve the mechanical advantage during the contraction. This helps to produce greater leverage.
5. The chemicals that aid in energy output, especially those along the nerve pathways like epinephrine (adrenalin), are liberated with greater ease.

These gains can only be brought about to any significant degree by the employment of the *Overload Principle* which is not difficult to understand if it is remembered that the body always overcompensates when under stress. The most dramatic example of overcompensation may be observed in noting the effect of a simple vaccination. The vaccination itself is only mildly toxic, but the body produces enough antibodies to fight a disease many times more ravaging.

In order to improve any component, strength, local-muscle-endurance, or cardiovascular endurance, it is necessary to subject the body to a stress slightly beyond its normal capacity. For example, by training with weights that are equal to the load normally lifted each day, only the same number of fibers will be employed. In fact, as skill improves, fewer numbers will be utilized. The body always strives for efficiency. However, by using a weight five or ten pounds beyond the usual load, more fibers are called upon to complete the lift. At first this confuses the pattern that the body has established. Nerve impulses are discharged wildly, more adrenalin than is necessary is rushed into the blood stream, and the heart and lungs work excessively to do their jobs. This reaction occurs even from a mild stress as long as it is beyond the individual's normal load.

Of course, within a few days the body *adapts* to this new stress. It no longer wastes nerve impulses, heart beats, or breaths, but uses only those that are needed to get the task done. However, now all these operations are being performed on a higher level than before (remember, the weight is ten pounds heavier), but with the same level of fatigue occurring. As a result, the body may be said to have a heightened capacity, in this case, more strength. By continuing then to increase the amount of weight in small dosages it is possible to increase the strength to great heights. Most people encounter a period of two or three weeks in which the "confusion" of the body actually makes them weaker than they were at the start. However, by persevering in the regular application of the Overload Principle the strength gains will come within a month or so. The application of this principle to not only weight-training, but to running and other exercise approaches, will be discussed in future chapters.

In summary, the exercise program that you devise should be geared to meeting the four basic components of fitness: cardiovascular endurance, flexibility, local-muscle-endurance, and muscle strength. Each component has a bearing on each of the others; however, it should be clear that certain unique phenomena define and describe each component. The conditioner who desires an optimal balanced physical fitness will keep them in mind.

References

1. H. A. DeVries, *Physiology of Exercise* (Dubuque, Iowa: Wm. C. Brown Company, 1966) p. 361.
2. D. K. Mathews, R. W. Stacy, and G. N. Hoover, *Exercise Physiology* (New York: The Ronald Press Company, 1964) p. 213.
3. *Ibid.*, p. 167.

4

Flexibility and Warm-Up: The First Steps to Fitness

In this chapter you will be introduced to various exercises that have been designed to increase your range of movement. The assumption is that you are "stiff" and inflexible to some degree at this time. Without beginning on that assumption you may incur an injury that would retard your program many weeks.

"Warming-up" has been a tradition long honored by most athletes. It has always been felt that the stretching of the limbs and the taking on of a "small sweat" were beneficial to the quality of performance and to the prevention of injuries. Recently certain researchers[1] have questioned whether or not this is true. Through well-controlled experiments they have been able to produce proof that warm-up neither benefits nor hinders endurance performances or the sustaining of injuries.

However, it is the suggestion of these scientists that the practice of warming-up be continued until more data are obtained. The point is to not delude yourself into great expectations simply because you have warmed-up. Rather, use the warm-up in its traditional sense simply to get your system started and to stretch yourself properly to avoid possible injury. The following outline suggests a combination of exercises that is usually adequate for these purposes.

EXERCISE	AMOUNT THE FIRST DAY
1. Slow jogging-in-place	15-20 seconds
2. Alternate Toe Touches (See Figure 11)	6 to each toe
3. Upper Trunk Twists (See Figure 7, p. 19)	5 to each side
4. Slow Deep Knee Bends (See Figure 12)	4-5
5. Shoulder Shrugs (See Figure 13)	10 rotations
6. Knees to Chest Hold (See Figure 14)	5 3-count holds
7. Chest Curl Situp (See Figure 15)	5 3-count holds
8. Finish with Side-Straddle Hops (See Figure 8, p. 19)	5 quickly

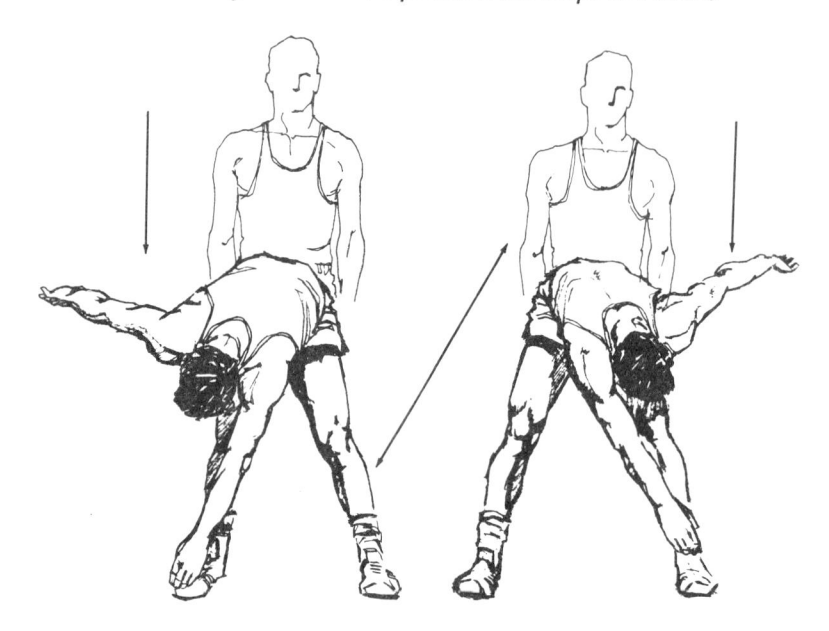

FIGURE 11. *Alternate Toe Touches*

FIGURE 12. *Slow Deep Knee Bends*

Flexibility and Warm-Up: The First Steps to Fitness   37

FIGURE 13.   *Shoulder Shrugs*

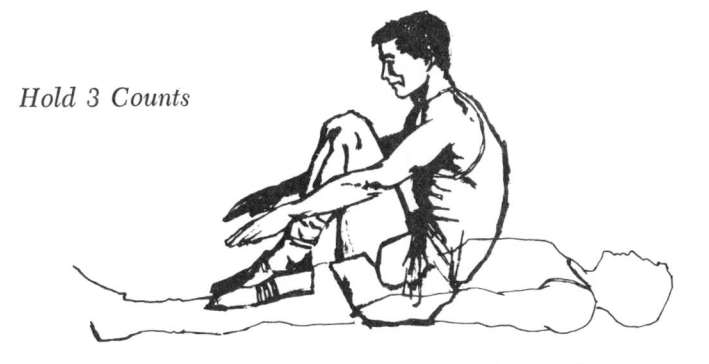

Hold 3 Counts

FIGURE 14.   *Knees To Chest Hold*

Exhale on the Rise
Hold 3 Counts

FIGURE 15.   *Chest Curl Situp*

38   *Flexibility and Warm-Up: The First Steps to Fitness*

The numbers suggested are for a first day workout and are minimal. However, even after you have improved your condition, it would not be sensible to increase these numbers by too many. After all, this is just the warm-up. Always do these initial exercises slowly. To promote flexibility in the safest way it is wise to perform the exercise slowly with a slight hold at the full extent of your range of motion.

The exercise suggestions that follow should be integrated into your total workout program. That is, once you have planned your cardio-

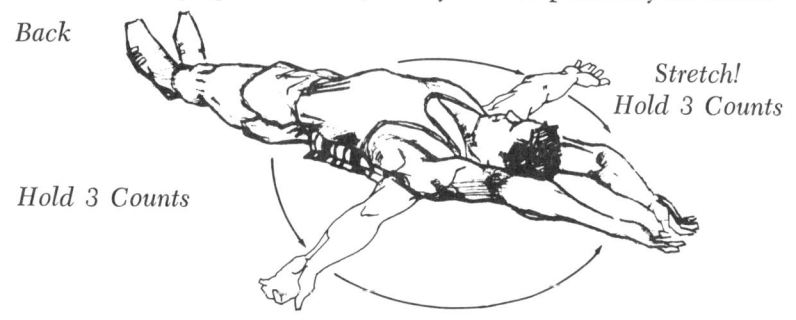

Back

Stretch!
Hold 3 Counts

Hold 3 Counts

FIGURE 16.   *Back Exercise A—Supine Arm Stretch with Towel*

FIGURE 17.   *Back Exercise B—Forward Bend and Circle Up*

Flexibility and Warm-Up: The First Steps to Fitness 39

vascular, local-muscle-endurance, and strength exercises, alternate these exercises to give you a "rest" or a break from the more strenuous ones. Also, because of the nature of weight-training work, a stretching action immediately following heavy weight work seems to reduce the chance of severe muscle cramping. The exercises in Figures 16-34 are shown in order of difficulty. Alternate the areas of the body that you exercise and build from least difficult to the most difficult.

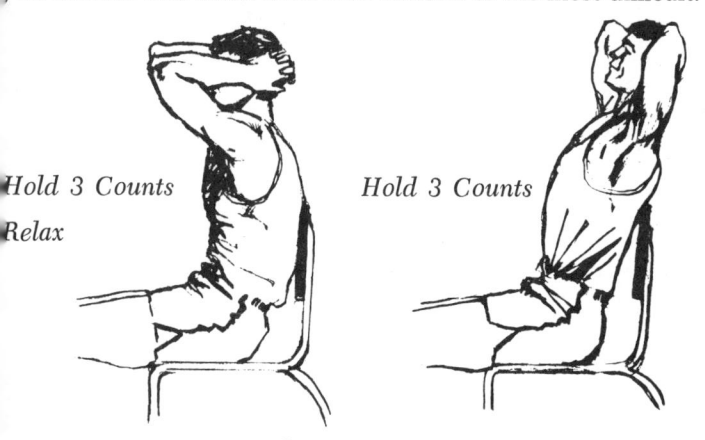

Hold 3 Counts
Relax

Hold 3 Counts

FIGURE 18. *Back Exercise C—Sitting and Stretching*

Slowly
nce slightly
full twist

FIGURE 19. *Back Exercise D—Upper Trunk Twist— Barbell Empty*

40   *Flexibility and Warm-Up: The First Steps to Fitness*

Do slowly in rhythm.

FIGURE 20.   *Back Exercise E—Sitting Forward Bend*

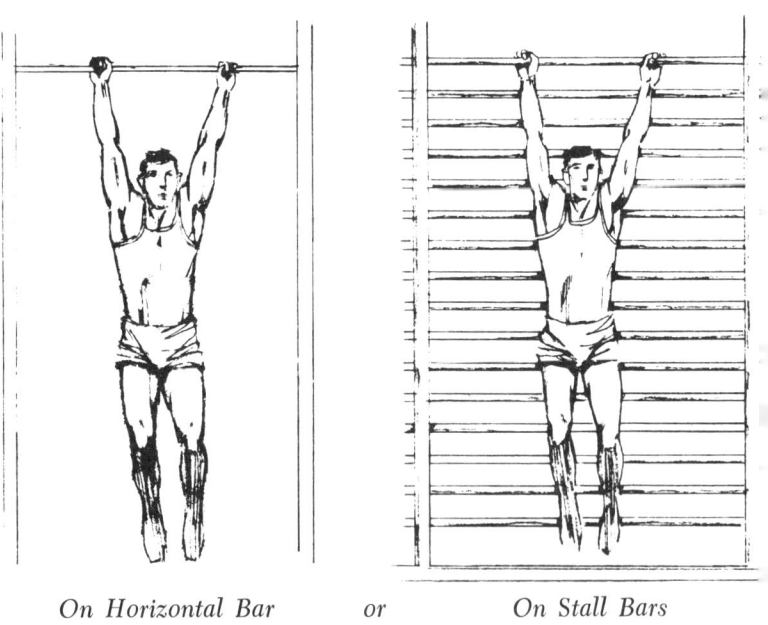

| On Horizontal Bar | or | On Stall Bars |
| Flex Knees Slightly | | Flatten Back against Bars |

Hang "passively" for five seconds. → *Get down and rest five seconds.* → *Hang "actively" (muscles contracted more, but not pulling) for five seconds.*

FIGURE 21.   *Back Exercise F—The Hanging Exercise*

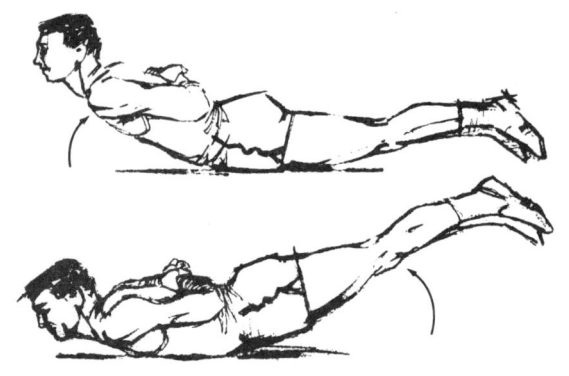

Flexibility and Warm-Up: The First Steps to Fitness   41

FIGURE 22.   Back Exercise G—Rocker

FIGURE 23.   Back Exercise H—Seal Raise

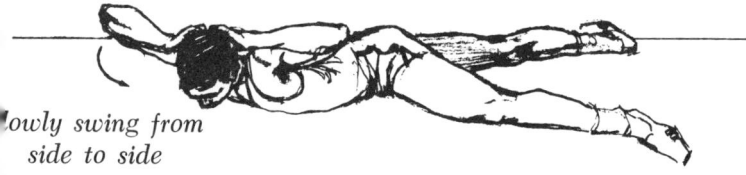

*owly swing from
side to side*

FIGURE 24.   Back Exercise I—Back Rotators

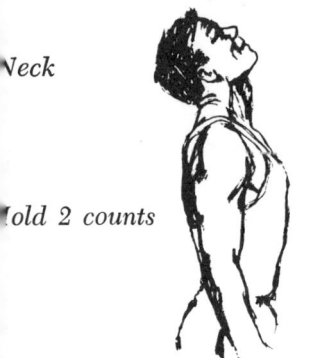

Neck

old 2 counts   *Hold 2 counts*

FIGURE 25.   Neck Exercise A—Head Nodding

Roll head slowly in clock-wise direction

Roll head slowly in counter-clockwise direction

FIGURE 26. Neck Exercise B—Neck Roll

Shoulders

*Hold 3 counts
Stretch fingers*

FIGURE 27. Shoulder Exercise A—Arm Raise and Stretch

FIGURE 28. Shoulder Exercise B—Standing Arm Circles

Flexibility and Warm-Up: The First Steps to Fitness 43

Hips and Thighs

  A. Starting Exercise: Alternate Toe Touches. See Figure 11, page 36. For Hamstrings area.
  B. Deep Knee Bends: See Figure 12, page 36. For Quadriceps area.
  C. Running in place—high knee raises. For general leg flexibility.

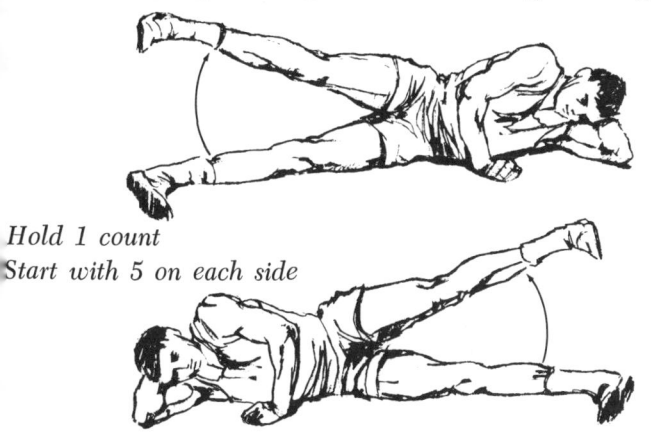

Hold 1 count
Start with 5 on each side

FIGURE 29. *Hip-Thigh Exercise D—Lying Leg Raises to Side*

Do not hold

FIGURE 30. *Hip-Thigh Exercise E—Alternate Leg Raise to Rear*

Hold-bobbing 2 counts

FIGURE 31. *Hip-Thigh Exercise F—Hurdle Stretch*

*Hold 2 counts
Be very careful*

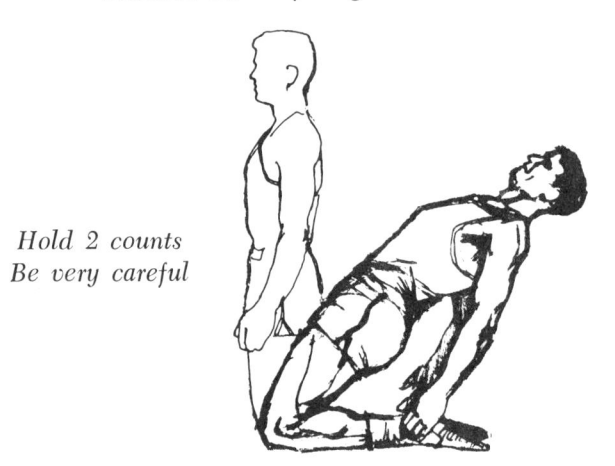

FIGURE 32. *Hip-Thigh Exercise G—Stiff Body Lean*

*Hold 2 counts
Do very slowly*

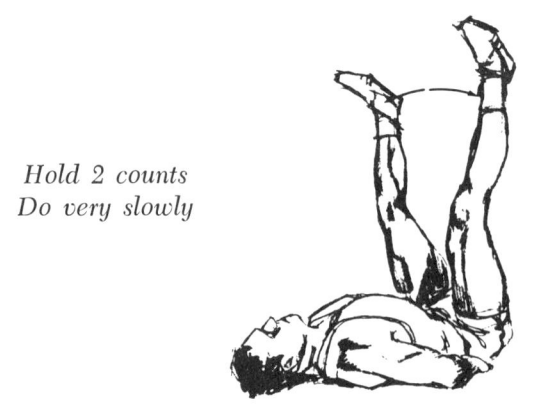

FIGURE 33. *Hip-Thigh Exercise H—Prone Leg Spread*

Flexibility and Warm-Up: The First Steps to Fitness 45

Hold 2 counts

FIGURE 34. *Hip-Thigh Exercise I—Fencer's Stretch*

The exercises mentioned here are just a few that can be used in the first step of your conditioning program. No matter what your condition may be, from middle-aged and breathless to eighteen and windy, it is vital that you begin with these kinds of exercises. The ones noted here are as good as any, and the sequence has been designed to cover almost every major muscle area of the body.

Two muscle areas that have been neglected are those of the lower legs and feet and abdominal area. The strength exercises for these areas are designed to promote both flexibility and strength. Therefore, many more exercises for these areas are listed in Chapter Six.

To summarize, flexibility is developed very readily in combination with strength training, and especially with weight-training. It is recommended that the flexibility exercises listed above be the primary workout for the first several weeks of your program along with some mild cardiovascular work. Then as you become more and more conditioned, it would be wise to integrate the flexibility exercises into the breaks between your other exercises.

Reference

Karpovich, *Physiology of Muscular Activity*, pp. 13-14.

5

Cardiovascular Fitness: The Foundational Step

The development of the heart muscle and the blood vessels is called the foundation of your fitness program simply because without it all other conditioning is retarded. The base for respiratory improvement, strength development, posture, local-muscle-endurance, muscle tone, or any fitness component is structured from a sound, efficient heart with elastic, active blood vessels supplying the tissues. Even the weight-lifters striving for Olympian strength work hard at developing this aspect through running and rope-skipping programs. No longer do the good lifters "just lift;" they run, too.

In this chapter are suggestions on how best to condition the cardiovascular-respiratory system. The appeal will be for a systematized approach; i.e., do not just run, or rope-skip, or do calisthenics by your whim of the moment. Set goals within your grasp for each day and achieve them. Then plan again, set new goals, and push yourself to meet them. Have something long-range in mind, but lay primary importance on meeting the immediate goals of each day. Sometimes one day of failure discourages people from continuing. It is imperative, therefore, that you plan wisely.

This is not to say that some "mood-running" is not advised. Very often, in order to break the monotony of order and system, a runner will just "hit the country-side" for some relaxation without thought of time or goals. The point is to include mood-running as a break in your program, not as the basis of it. The reason for this advice lies in understanding the nature of men. Most men have trouble pushing themselves to the point of stress that will truly help them. Without a system of goal-setting, they stop at their first feeling of fatigue. By systematizing these fatigue warnings, it is easier to know which ones to obey and which ones to push through. It is from this psychological base that the system of conditioning popularly known as *Interval Training* gets its real value.

Interval Training

Perhaps the most amazing approach to conditioning of the past forty years has been Interval Training. For many years athletes used a form of this system on a more or less trial and error basis. One example was in the use of "wind sprints." Runners would run at various speeds for different lengths according to their mood of the moment. In the Scandinavian countries this approach was called "fartlek," and is still used by some marathon runners.

However, just prior to World War II some runners began to systematize their training. Emil Zatopek, the Czech distance runner, refined his program for a number of years and reportedly used the following system as part of his preparation to run the 5000 meters in the 1948 Olympics: (1) He ran sixty 400 meter runs at 60-75 second pace; (2) he alternated these with sixty 200 meter jogs at about a 60-second pace. This he did for ten days in succession prior to the Games. In 1952 he won three gold medals at different distances, and his program was as follows: (1) He ran twenty 200 meter trots at a 34-second pace; (2) he alternated these with forty 400 meter runs at a 75-90 second pace; (3) he would alternate the fast intervals with 200 meter jogs at a 60 second pace.[1] This same Zatopek used to walk holding his breath until he fainted in order to get used to an oxygen lack. This kind of dedication is both unusual and dangerous. The point is that his planning drove him and his body to unbelievable heights of physical condition. That other humans can approximate his achievements within the limits of their own organisms is a perfectly rational conclusion to be drawn from Zatopek's example; however, no one would expect the average person to set up such a schedule.

From Zatopek's program it is possible to observe the variables of an interval program in running: (1) Length of time of work interval; (2) work rate during work interval; (3) length of time of rest interval; (4) work rate during rest interval; (5) repetitions of work interval; (6) periodicity of workouts (say, the number of days between workouts); (7) the terrain (a factor when a track or gym is not consistently available).

Since World War II many "systems" of interval training have evolved for use in running and swimming. The programs today stress "quality" running as much as the kind of "quantity" training that Zatopek did. To keep this difference simple, think of it in terms of the goal that one has in beginning training in the first place. If one wished to train for faster times in the hundred-yard dash, he would embark on a different program than if his goal were to run a five minute mile.

In a conditioning program for the average person the planning should start with an intermediate goal and later evolve towards a different goal of greater or lesser distance, or faster speeds. This means that one might set as a goal the time of 2:40 in the half-mile. Once this goal is achieved a new goal of a six-minute mile, or a goal of faster 100-yard dash times could be established. The goal would relate to the kind of activity in which one has an interest. Skill in basketball involves a somewhat different kind of endurance than that needed for the sport of hiking. Both involve training for cardiovascular fitness, but each has its own special demands.

Just as in all other phases of conditioning, the Overload Principle is the key. The cardiovascular system, just as with a single muscle, must be given a stress slightly beyond the normal to which it can and will adapt. The form of the adaptation depends upon the nature of the stress. For example, if one's goal is to be able to run or walk for long distances without tiring he needs to be able to utilize his oxygen more and more efficiently; as one's oxygen utilization improves, his distance running can increase, and the times for each distance should go down. The reason is easy to see. By conditioning the body to take in more air with each inspiration, to distribute this oxygen to the tissues more rapidly, and to resynthesize and eliminate the waste products more readily, it is possible to ward off fatigue longer. Therefore, the conditioner can run farther, thus accomplishing his goal.

To improve *oxygen utilization* most track coaches recommend for the beginner a program somewhat similar to the following:

1. Spend two weeks to a month in *quantity* running—jogging slowly at first for a quarter mile and building to a mile or mile and a half by the end of the month.

2. After a month or so, set a goal, say a 2:40 half-mile.

3. Warm-up each day with a quarter-mile jog.

4. Select variables of about one-fourth the objective and begin progressive program somewhat as follows:

Cardiovascular Fitness: The Foundational Step

GOAL: 2:40 Half-mile

	Distance	Time	Time of rest	Activity in rest	Repetitions	Days rest
1st Day	220 yds.	35–40 secs.	120 secs.	Walk	8	1
2nd Day	"	"	"	"	9	1
3rd Day	"	"	"	"	10	1
4th Day	"	"	80 secs.	"	10	2
5th Day	"	"	60 secs.	"	10	1
6th Day	"	"	45 secs.	"	10	1
7th Day	"	35 secs.	45 secs.	"	10	1
8th Day	"	"	35 secs.	"	10	2
9th Day	"	"	30 secs.	"	9	1
.	.	.	.	.	.	.
.	.	.	.	.	.	.
? Day	220 yds.	35 secs.	10 secs.	Walk	4	1
? Day	220 yds.	40 secs.	5 secs.	Walk	4	1
Goal Day	220 yds.	40 secs.	0	None	4	

In reading this chart note the similarities from day to day along with the differences. For example, only the "Repetitions" variable changes in the first of these days. Then after an extra day of rest, a change is made on the fourth day in the "Time or rest" variable. As this is reduced, the "Time" variable is stabilized. Soon, according to your ability, all the variables have adjusted to enable you to run the half-mile in 160 seconds, or 2:40.

The "Time" variable indicates the number of seconds under which all repetitions will be run. This program is simply an example of how one might go about using the variables of an Interval Training program to build toward a specific goal. You most certainly would want to vary it to fit your time schedule and capacities. The degree of change each day will vary from person to person, but remember to make only small changes in one or two variables at the most. A failure can disintegrate one's will to continue.

From such a start you might wish to set a new goal, say a faster 100-yard dash time. For people who enjoy such sports as basketball, tennis, or even hockey, this new goal might prove beneficial.

In sprinting one uses oxygen very quickly, far faster than in a distance jog. So for most of the sprint a person operates without oxygen entering the body. Previously in Chapter Three, you were introduced to the phenomenon of a muscle working without oxygen. The term used to denote this physiological occurrence is *oxygen debt*. Like any other stress the body can be trained to adapt to it. A conditioner needs to learn to tolerate a quick depletion of oxygen to his system as well as to learn to dissipate the effects quickly afterwards.

Track coaches usually advise that a man continue with the kind of program used for the 2:40 half-mile, but begin tacking on Repetition Sprints at the end in order to train for this kind of stress. A good beginning for a person fit enough to run a 2:40 half-mile might be the following:

	Distance	Time	Time of rest	Activity in rest	Repetition
1st Day	40 yds.	6 secs.	15 secs.	Slow Jog	5
2nd Day	100 yds.	15 secs.	45 secs.	"	4
3rd Day	40 yds.	6 secs.	15 secs.	"	6
4th Day	70 yds.	10 secs.	30 secs.	"	5
5th Day	40 yds.	6 secs.	15 secs.	"	7

Dr. Richard Bowers, Assistant Professor in The Ohio State University Physical Education Department, provided the author with these sample programs.

Again, this is just a sample of what you might employ to increase your sprint speed and endurance. The distances are not magic, nor are any of the other variable designations. The changes are made in the name of variety, not because any research has deigned that these increments be used. The important factor is that an all-out effort be made, and greater distances would probably mean less than all-out.

Only through an all-out effort can the conditioner cause his body to experience a very curious phenomenon. Not all physiologists agree on the details, but for the most part it has been determined that if the exercise is strenuous enough the heart pumps more blood per beat in the immediate five to thirty seconds right after cessation of exercise than during the work itself.[2] This tends to open up previously unused capillaries in the heart and muscle areas, and to stretch the vessels so that they are bigger and more elastic. The body, in essence, has taken on a new, improved capacity. If the exercise is not vigorous enough this phenomenon does not occur. Also, if after thirty-seconds or so the conditioner ceases moving, the gains are nullified somewhat. It is necessary to train in intervals of hard work, brief rest, hard work, brief rest, and so on, stopping when the fatigue begins to affect significantly the "Time" variable. This is usually a good signal that it is time for a lengthier rest.

It is for these reasons that simple jogging after the first month or so loses its value as a total conditioner of the cardiovascular system. Once the body has adapted to the jogging, the stress is reduced to the point where the phenomenon of higher stroke production of blood by the heart during rest does not occur. Without this happening the body cannot develop further efficiency. This accounts, in part, for the plateau that some conditioners reach in which they cannot seem to make any higher goals. Again, this non-attainment is psychologically debilitating. It can cause the conditioner to stop working.

Of course, there is another kind of plateau to consider. Eventually you will reach a peak of performance beyond which it would be dangerous to push yourself. This is strictly a physiological limitation and must be obeyed. By changing the program only slightly each day this limit is easily recognized, and the danger of excess fatigue is avoided.

Some conditioners may wish to go on from the 2:40 half-mile to build better times at a greater distance. Following is a program which might be used as a guideline for this interest:

GOAL: 6:00 Mile

	Distance	Time	Time of rest	Activity in rest	Repetitions
1st Day	440 yds.	90 secs.	120 secs.	Walk	3
2nd Day	"	"	"	"	4
.	.	.	.	.	.
? Day	440 yds.	"	60 secs.	"	4
? Day	"	"	50 secs.	"	"
.	.	.	.	.	.
? Day	440 yds.	90 secs.	10 secs.	Walk-Jog	4
Goal Day	440 yds.	90 secs.	0	None	4

Even faster times in the mile could be achieved by using the above program and lowering the "Time" variable a little each day.

Whatever goal you decide upon remember the two specific cardio-vascular-respiratory gains which dictate your approach:

1. Improvement in oxygen intake and oxygen utilization. This is the primary need of all distance runners.
2. Improvement in ability to tolerate and dissipate the oxygen debt. This is the primary need of all sprinters.

One caution is needed: conditioning is specific. There is not as much carry-over from one activity to another as fitness buffs like to think. To run on a track in training for basketball is not anywhere near as valuable, nor as quick a conditioner, as simply playing the game itself on a regular, vigorous basis. However, by approximating the demands involved in the game the conditioner can provide a better foundation for the time when he finally gets a chance to play the sport.

A training system that utilizes exercises for strength, flexibility, local-muscle-endurance, and other such components has become quite popular in recent years. It stresses the body similarly to the interval training approach and is known as circuit training.

Circuit Training

Circuit training seems to be many things to many people. In recent years some trainers have used the phrase only when the circuit of exercises involved all of the fitness components. However, some people have devised circuits that have one specific goal, like strength, or cardiovascular development, or just flexibility.

The key factor is that the arrangement of the exercises should be such that *three* variables are utilized to provide a progressive workout. Sorani feels that other types of conditioning utilize only two variables. In weight training one varies the *load* and the *repetitions*. In interval running one varies the *repetitions* and the *time*.[3] Thus if one devises a program utilizing variances in all three, repetitions, weight-load, and time, he may be said to be engaged in some form of circuit training.

The advantages of most of the circuits now in use are these:

1. Circuit programs are very adaptable, easily modified to men, women, or children.
2. They can be employed by large groups or individuals with equal ease.
3. They are excellent for adaptation to time limitations.
4. Expensive equipment is not needed.
5. Progression is systematized to account for individual needs.
6. Motivation is built-in by the variety of the circuit and the reasonableness of the goals.[4]

Cardiovascular Fitness: The Foundational Step

The only disadvantages are inherent in its advantages. That is, its flexibility is possible only at the expense of specialization. As you will read in the next chapter, weight-training requires concentrated effort without the spectre of a time limit in order to achieve optimal strength development. And, as you have read in this chapter, cardio-respiratory gains can only be optimal if the stress is great. Circuits necessarily spread the stress over the entire series of exercises to develop all-around fitness. Even with such drawbacks, it may be that you are more interested in a short, somewhat vigorous bout of exercise than you are in the complete development of any one component. For this kind of goal, circuit training may prove interesting.

Perhaps the two most used "circuits" these days are the 5BX program for men devised by the Royal Canadian Air Force, and the Official United States Physical Fitness Program prepared by the President's Council on Physical Fitness. These two programs are very similar and both promise fitness in just a few minutes a day.

Figure 35 relates the way in which the simplest or beginning level for the 5BX plan is arranged. The half-mile run or one-mile walk are extras to the basic five exercises. The basic five are to be done in no more than eleven minutes. By starting with Chart 1, at D-Level, a conditioner may proceed through to the A+ Level and move on to Chart 2. There are six charts with a total of seventy-two levels. The exercises vary slightly as the levels get tougher.

This program is highly recommended for three types of conditioners: (1) The conditioner who is extremely busy and can devote only ten to fifteen minutes a day to his fitness; or (2) the regular conditioner who uses it as a starting program for about a month or so and hopes to have more time to devote to conditioning eventually; or (3) the athlete who uses it as an off-season program. Both this program and the United States Program can be obtained through booklets selling at most magazine stands.

One of the best programs now in use is called the Modified U.S.C. Circuit, devised at the University of Southern California. Table 5 outlines that program to give you an example of a widely used circuit. The Red circuit is the starting level and the Blue circuit is the more advanced one. The conditioner attempts to go through the eleven exercises as prescribed three times in twenty-three minutes (twenty-five minutes for the Blue circuit). This circuit requires equipment and weight-training knowledge. It would be wise, therefore, to read the

54   *Cardiovascular Fitness: The Foundational Step*

next chapter before attempting to use it. Many circuits use isometric exercises in place of weight-training for development of the strength component. This is highly recommended and will be explained in the next chapter.

Exercise 1

Exercise 2

Exercise 3

Exercise 4

Exercise 5

FIGURE 35. *Sample of Beginning Level—5BX Plan*

Cardiovascular Fitness: The Foundational Step

PHYSICAL CAPACITY RATING SCALE

Level	EXERCISE 1	2	3	4	5	½ mile run	1 mile walk
					In Minutes		
A+	20	18	22	13	400	5½	17
A	18	17	20	12	375	5½	17
A−	16	15	18	11	335	5½	17
B+	14	13	16	8	320	6	18
B	12	12	14	8	305	6	18
B−	10	11	12	7	280	6	18
C+	8	9	10	6	260	6½	19
C	7	8	9	5	235	6½	19
C−	6	7	8	4	205	6½	19
D+	4	5	6	3	175	7	20
D	3	4	5	3	145	7½	21
D−	2	3	4	3	188	8	21
Minutes for each exercise	2	.1	1	1	8		

AGE GROUPS
6 YRS. MAINTAINS B
7 YRS. MAINTAINS A

CHART I—

1 Feet astride, arms upward.
—Forward bend to floor touching then stretch upward and backward bend.
—Do not strain to keep knees straight.

2 Back lying, feet 6" apart, arms at sides.
—Sit up just far enough to see your heels.
—Keep legs straight, head and shoulders must clear the floor.

3 Front lying, palms placed under the thighs.
—Raise head and one leg, repeat using legs alternately.
—Keep leg straight at the knee, thighs must clear the palms.
(Count one each time second leg touches floor.)

4 Front lying, hands under the shoulders, palms flat on the floor.
—Straighten arms lifting upper body, keeping the knees on the floor. Bend arms to lower body.
—Keep body straight from the knees, arms must be fully extended, chest must touch floor to complete one movement.

5 **Stationary run**—(Count a step each time left foot touches floor.) Lift feet approximately 4 inches off floor. Every 75 steps do 10 "scissor jumps." Repeat this sequence until required number of steps is completed.

Scissor jumps—Stand with right leg and left arm extended forward, and left leg and right arm extended backward.

Jump up—change position of arms and legs before landing. Repeat (arms shoulder high).

Chart reprinted by permission of Pocket Books, Inc., and *This Week* magazine, through the Crown Copyright of Canada, *Royal Canadian Air Force Exercise Plans for Physical Fitness*, 1962, pp. 68-69.

TABLE 5

Modified U.S.C. Circuit

Target Times		Red—23 minutes			Blue—25 minutes			
		RED CIRCUIT				BLUE CIRCUIT		
No.	Exercises	Wt.	1	2	3	Wt.	1	2	3
1. Bench press		60#	8	10	12	80#	8	10	12
2. Back shuffle			7	9	11		13	15	17
3. Chins			1	3	5		7	9	10
4. Back extension			7	9	12	10#	9	12	14
5. Ladder (bent arm)			3	5	7		9	12	15*
6. Squat thrust			10	13	16		19	22	25
7. Curl sit-ups (bent leg)			15	20	25	10#	15	20	25
8. Two-arm curl		45#	8	10	12	55#	8	10	12
9. Three-quarter squat		75#	9	12	15	95#	12	14	16
10. Bent lateral raise		2x8#	8	10	12	2x12#	8	10	12
11. Stair climb			4	6	8	12#	8	10	12†

* Rungs
† Flights

R. P. Sorani, *Circuit Training* (Dubuque, Iowa: Wm. C. Brown Co., 1966) p. 40.

References

1. W. W. Heusner, "Specificity of Interval Training," East Lansing, Michigan: Michigan State University, 1963.
2. *Ibid.*, p. 4.
3. R. P. Sorani, *Circuit Training* (Dubuque, Iowa: Wm. C. Brown Co. 1966) p. 5.
4. *Ibid.*, pp. 4-6.

6
Building Muscles

This chapter will acquaint you with some ideas to help develop muscle strength, local-muscle-endurance, muscle power, muscle tone, and muscle coordination. The focus of information will be on weight-training and isometric exercise programs because they are the most efficient and effective approaches to muscle building.

The muscle can be made to work in three ways, isotonically, isometrically, or eccentrically. The differences in these types of contraction need to be understood if you intend to design your own program. An *isotonic* contraction is one where the muscle fibers shorten during the work. Figure 36 illustrates the biceps brachii performing isotonically during the two-arm curl.

FIGURE 36. *Two Arm Curl—Isotonic Contraction*

An *isometric* contraction is one where the muscle fibers receive the nerve stimulation and all the intra-muscle metabolism is initiated, but because of the nature of the resistance there is no shortening of the fibers. Figure 37 illustrates the biceps brachii performing isometrically against an immovable resistance.

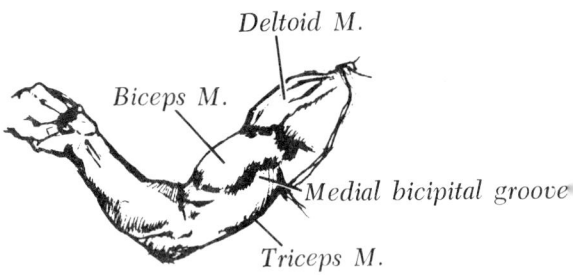

FIGURE 37. *Two Arm Curl—Isometric Contraction*

An *eccentric* contraction is similar to the isotonic in that there are changes in the lengths of the muscle fibers. The difference is that the fibers are being lengthened rather than shortened. Usually this type of work is done *with* gravity, slowly. Figure 38 illustrates the biceps brachii slowly lowering the barbell during a two-arm curl. If the barbell were quickly lowered no muscle action of any consequence would be involved; gravity would be responsible for the action. However, by slowly lowering the barbell the fibers of the biceps brachii muscle are forced into employment and the actual lengthening of them becomes an active exercise rather than a passive one.

FIGURE 38. *Two Arm Curl—Eccentric Contraction*

Weight-training employs isotonic and eccentric contractions since the muscle fibers either shorten or lengthen to bring about movement of the weight. The famed "dynamic tension" exercises of Charles Atlas are really isometric exercises since no movement is involved. Perhaps a more accurate term for these exercises, although less commercial, would be static exercises. In planning your muscle building program it would be wise to utilize all three types of contraction with the primary emphasis placed on isotonic and isometric work.

Muscle Strength

The best approach to developing this factor is through the use of a daily isometric program and a weight-training program done every other day. Ten or twelve isometric exercises should be chosen with the idea of working all major muscle groups. The average person can almost "create" his own isometric program. Simply look around your room or home for some immovable objects, like a doorway, a heavy desk, a wall, a floor, your wife or husband, to name several. By exerting pressure against these items you involve yourself in isometric exercise. With a little reasoning you should then be able to discern the muscle area being used.

The research is almost unanimous in its opinion that isometric contractions done on a regular basis build pure strength faster than any other method, weight-training included. What is not altogether established is the time and number of sets per day. Highly respected laboratories, however, suggest the following:

1. Hold the contraction for six seconds.
2. Do it at about two-thirds of all-out effort.
3. Do only one set per day, but do at least the one set every day.[1]

It is difficult to judge "two-thirds effort," but the point is that you need not strain to the point of pain to get benefit from isometric work. If you understand the idea behind a "point of diminishing returns" it will probably not be too difficult to understand these laboratory findings and recommendations. Longer contractions and more sets per day are simply a waste of your time.

The time would be more wisely spent engaged in weight-training (with running on the odd days as outlined in Chapter Five). To build pure strength through weight-training, it is necessary to stress the muscles as the isometric exercises do. That is, a heavy load must be the resistance and the number of repetitions must be few. Of course, in isometric work the number of repetitions is zero. *Repetitions* simply mean the number of executions of the movement in any one continuous effort. *Sets* mean the number of different times in a workout that a particular exercise is done.

Competitive weight-lifters have as their primary goal to build pure strength, and so it is from them that we have learned the best approach. Usually they warm-up utilizing some calisthenics and light lifting. But once they begin to concentrate on the strength building certain guidelines are followed:

1. Use weights heavy enough that no more than four to five repetitions are possible in any one set.
2. Add weight with each set so that less repetitions are possible.
3. The last set, usually the fifth or sixth, should be weighted such that only one or two repetitions are possible.
4. Once a week use a weight for which only one repetition is possible.

Some weight-lifters vary this guide to overcome certain psychological barriers which accrue from any routine. Instead of working every other day some men lift for two consecutive days and rest the third which may involve the split-training routine. In this method the first day involves exercises for the legs, chest, shoulders, and abdominal areas. The second day involves exercises for the upper and lower back, the arms, forearms, and neck. In this approach it is possible to devote more time and effort to specific muscle areas.

Local-Muscle-Endurance

Local-muscle-endurance, explained in detail in Chapter Three, emphasizes promoting optimal physical health in training for both pure strength and muscle endurance. Since the average person does not have time to do both separately, he must utilize approaches that get at both factors in a reasonable time period. For that reason the following guidelines in using weights are offered to anyone other than the competitive weight-lifter (assuming proper warm-up and cardiovascular work):

1. Utilize a weight-load for the first set of an exercise, which is just heavy enough, so that you can make no more than ten to twelve repetitions.
2. Do not do a second set of the same exercise for at least five minutes. Do other exercises which do not engage the same muscle area.
3. Add just enough weight for the second set that you can make no more than eight or nine repetitions.
4. After a proper interval do a last set in which the weight used is such that you can make no more than six or seven repetitions.
5. Once every two weeks use a weight heavy enough that on your last set it is impossible for you to make more than three repetitions.

These five points outline the best approach for the average person. Through them, it is possible to develop strength, local-muscle-endurance, and with some variations, muscle power in an interesting, effective manner.

Muscle Power

Muscle power is defined as the ability to apply force with speed. It is considered a key factor in athletic ability. The problem in developing muscle power is that the arrangement of the muscles to the bones is a lever situation. Without getting into physical principles too deeply, let us say that is extremely difficult to have both force and speed of application at the same time within any one muscle action. The relationships between the force arm, the fulcrum, and the resistance or weight arm are illustrated in Figure 39.

Most of the muscles of the body are third class levers; i.e., the force arm, or point at which tension is applied, is closer to the fulcrum (the joint) than the resistance or weight-load. As a result, power is sacrificed for speed and range of movement. An important exception to this is in the calf area, one of the few first class levers in the body, where the lever arrangement is such that the power is greater. This is why the standing broad jump and the vertical jump are considered excellent measures of muscle power.

Thus, to develop muscle power in most muscles of the body is not easy but requires the use of resistances heavy enough to need great

1st Class

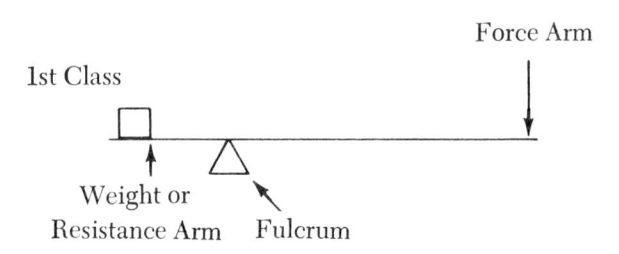

```
                              Force Arm
                                  ↓
        ┌─┐
        └─┘─────────△──────────────
         ↑         
    Weight or    Fulcrum
    Resistance Arm
```

1st Class : *Fulcrum* between the *Force* and the *Resistance*.
  A. If Force is applied further from the Fulcrum than the Resistance, *power* is gained, *speed* and *range* of movement are sacrificed. Calf muscles.
  B. If Force is applied nearer to Fulcrum than Resistance, the *speed* and *range* are increased, *power* reduced. Triceps muscle.

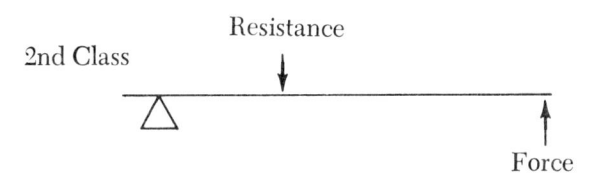

2nd Class

```
                    Resistance
                         ↓
    ─────△──────────────────────────
                                  ↑
                                Force
```

2nd Class : *Resistance* between the *Fulcrum* and the *Force*.
  Almost no muscles in human body have this arrangement. The wheelbarrow operates on this principle. Speed is sacrificed for power.

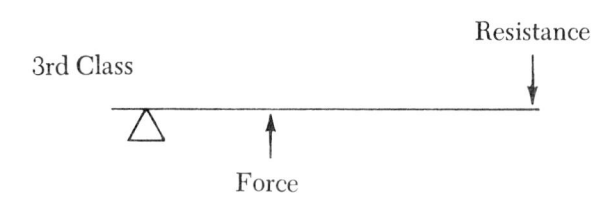

3rd Class

```
                                Resistance
                                    ↓
    ───△─────────↑──────────────────
                Force
```

3rd Class : *Force* applied between *Fulcrum* and *Resistance*.
  Shorter Force arm sacrifices *power* for *speed* and *range* of movement. Most human muscles are of this type.

FIGURE 39. *Three Classes of Levers*

force (strength), but not so heavy that the resistance cannot be lifted quickly. Obviously, it would be possible to incur great injury from a miscalculation of the resistance. However, weight-lifters feel that weights heavy enough to be lifted eight to twelve times are safe, yet provide enough resistance to develop power.

It is suggested, therefore, that one of the three sets that you use in your weight-training program be employed to develop muscle power. Certain so-called power exercises are suggested as well. The muscle power set is performed by making *power thrusts* with the weight. Power thrusts indicate that during the primary work the weight is moved quickly to the full extent rather than with moderate speed. The loss of moderate rhythm negates some of the capillarization that is desired for the development of local-muscle-endurance, but if power is to be improved this is necessary.

This points up the reasons for recommending three sets of the better exercises. The first set, involving ten to twelve repetitions, develops local-muscle-endurance through its mild resistance, rhythmical execution, and relatively high repetitions. The second set, involving eight or nine repetitions, develops strength and speed (power) through its moderately heavy resistance and thrusting execution. The third set, involving six or seven repetitions, develops strength and some local-muscle-endurance through its heavy resistance and slow execution.

Muscle Tone

As people get older their concerns in terms of muscles change from strength and power to a desire to simply not be debilated by muscle inadequacies. The idea of being bent-over and moving in a slow and jerky fashion does great damage to the psyche of any older person. There may be pathological reasons for these things occurring, such as a stroke. But for the most part, erect posture and firm muscle appearance are attributable to a muscle phenomenon known as *muscle tone.*

While most physiologists feel that muscle tone is a nebulous concept about which more research is needed, it seems to be generally conceded that the muscles seem to exist in a state of semi-contraction; i.e., due to some factor there is always enough nerve stimulation rotating among the muscle fibers that a little bit of energy is being released that causes a slight tension. In a positive sense this may be thought of as a readiness for action. What the factor is that causes this nervous stimulation is not clear. It may not exist; the thing now called muscle tone may only be a fluid level and not an electrical accretion.

However, there seems to be a relativeness about muscle tone that can be observed. There are no normal levels, but unused muscles display less firmness and seem to offer less support to the skeleton than exercised ones. Strength exercises provide the only approach to full utilization of all muscle fibers. As you learned in Chapter Three it is only during heavy resistance that the body employs all the muscle fibers. It therefore follows that the best way to improve muscle tone is through the kind of weight-training and isometric program recommended in this chapter.

Muscle Coordination

Many people do not associate weight-training with coordinated muscle movement. The picture of the thickly muscled weight-lifter at the carnival is probably partly responsible for this oversight. The facts are that strength and coordination are highly correlated. Studies have consistently shown that among adolescents and champion athletes the stronger performer is more often the most skilled in the sport. The fact that local-muscle-endurance is usually developed right along with strength implies that fatigue is not as destructive to the stronger man. Coordination is quickly destroyed when the products of fatigue overtake the muscles.

But even in the quality of performance the strong man does better. Speed of limb movement has been correlated directly with strength.[2] Agility and muscle power have been found to be dependent on strength.[3]

Coordination implies a harmonious combining of forces. In regard to the muscles of the body this may best be observed in the pairing of muscle groups, some muscles helping other muscles to cause movement. For example, in the flexion of the forearm, the biceps brachii muscle is the prime mover, but it receives help from the brachialis and the brachioradialis. Only during heavy resistance work are all of these muscles employed fully. They "learn" over a period of time to work together better because of the repetitions of fairly heavy weight-training.

Some muscle pairs work *antagonistically*, which is of great value to coordinated movement. If a muscle is stretched, a nervous reaction occurs called the *stretch reflex*, a concept introduced in Chapter Four. Since most muscles attach at a joint the stretch reflex can be stimulated by another muscle on the other side of the joint. For example, the biceps brachii contracts to flex the forearm at the elbow joint; the triceps tendon is stretched by this action since it is attached to that same elbow joint from the opposite side. The nerve impulse is relayed to the spinal cord and immediately an impulse returns to the triceps. The triceps is then chemically *inhibited* or *contracted* depending upon the type of action made by the biceps brachii. Of course, this is really a difference in degree, not kind. The inhibition is simply a lesser contraction rather than any complete relaxation.

This reflex arc is a complex process and is not outlined in detail in this book. The important factor in terms of muscle coordination is that the antagonist muscles must be "educated" to work narmoniously with the prime movers. This is where practice in a movement brings about a more coordinated performance. The first time that a person tries a skill it is usually jerky and somewhat clumsy, partly because the antagonist muscles have not yet "learned" the appropriate response, relative tension or relative inhibition. After repeatedly doing the movement this is finally mastered and a smooth action is executed. The smoothness itself adds to the degree of inhibition involved. It is thought that this learned inhibitory response may account for the high correlation between strength, flexibility, and coordination.

This development of coordination can be observed in the awkward way in which an infant flexes his elbow joint to bring a spoon to his mouth compared to the smoothness with which an adult does this. All skills are dependent upon the development of this kind of cooperation among the muscles.

Simple posture is maintained because of the stretch reflex. When the body falls forward the extensor muscles of the back and legs are stretched. They are activated rather than inhibited as a result of the jerking forward and proceed to contract, thus resisting the flexor muscles and the pull of gravity. The body is able, therefore, to maintain an upright position.

One direct way in which you could observe the stretch reflex would be to attempt to raise your leg from a supine position and keep your knee from bending. It is almost impossible because of the stretch reflex. As the leg rises the hamstring muscles on the back of the thigh are stretched. At a certain point they will pull on the lower leg causing it to bend about the knee.

This kind of information should enable you to more wisely design your exercise program. If nothing else, you should now realize the value of developing all of the muscles of the body to promote an integrated system of operation.

How To Select Your Exercises

Two vital considerations for any conditioner to make in his planning are: (1) Select exercises which meet your individual needs and goals. (2) Keep in mind the idea of providing a balanced program, one which exercises all the body areas to some degree. After these two paramount considerations have been made, and if time is available, the conditioner can begin catering to his interests. He should begin a search for activities and exercises that provide variety and challenge, and, thereby, are motivating to continued regular participation. This would include sports and games, swimming, more advanced weight-lifting, or any of a variety of activities that involve vigorous movement.

In Chapter Two a method for evaluating your physical needs was discussed. Hopefully, you are now cognizant of your weaknesses and strengths. It is less difficult to relate cardiovascular-respiratory weaknesses to exercises which would improve them than to relate muscle weaknesses to their respective exercises because it is not easy to pinpoint the exact muscle area that is responsible for the weakness. In the suggestions that follow, you will be informed about some matters pertinent to the exercise which should enable you to select more intelligently. You will find a drawing of the exercise and the action involved. Directions, benefits of the exercise, and other important information will accompany the drawing.

Primary muscles is simply a term indicating the principal muscles involved in the movement. It is almost impossible to isolate one muscle for any particular exercise, but the true value of weight-training is brought forth in the attempt to achieve relative isolation. Through proper form, a conditioner lifting weights can place a relatively large degree of stress on one particular muscle area, and at the same time relegate other muscle areas to secondary roles. Strength and endurance are built much more effectively by this kind of specialization and isolation of muscle areas.

The secondary roles of antagonism, cooperation (synergism), and neutralization are not to be downgraded. You have already seen how the first two are important; a *neutralizing* muscle is simply a stabilizer of the skeleton. For example, in doing a military press certain neutralizing muscles keep the back straight; or, in many arm movements certain neutralizing muscles contract to hold the humerus (upper arm bone) into its socket at the shoulder. These neutralizers are extremely important in preventing injury.

However, in choosing an exercise it is impossible to select on any basis other than to meet the needs of the primary muscles. If enough exercises are selected to stress all the key muscle areas, the secondary roles of other muscles will be fulfilled. For example, chinups are placed in a program because of their benefit to the biceps brachii and the latissimus dorsi muscles (the large back muscles attaching on the front of the arm).

The fact that the shoulder muscles (the deltoids) contract eccentrically during the exercise, or that four or five other muscles in the shoulder and chest area are contracting as neutralizers, or that the abdominal muscles and muscles around the spinal cord are serving as stabilizers to a straight back, is superfluous to the *planning* of the exercise program. Those muscles can be exercised later in specific exercises designed with them in mind as the *primary* muscles.

The notations on the drawings of each exercise are designed to help you know the primary muscle areas involved. However, it is not extremely difficult to figure these areas on your own. Think of stretching a rubber band between the different bones. By pulling on the rubber band it would be possible to shorten the distance between the bones. This is exactly how a muscle works. The only difference is in the sophisticated manner in which nature has stretched the muscles across joints. The use of the bone protuberances at the joint as a fulcrum is a good example of the amazing engineering of the body.

Figure 40 illustrates how one might apply the rubber band idea to the problem of recognizing primary muscles. It is not too difficult to convert from your reasoning in placing the rubber band to the area on the body where nature placed the muscle.

Logical placement of rubber band

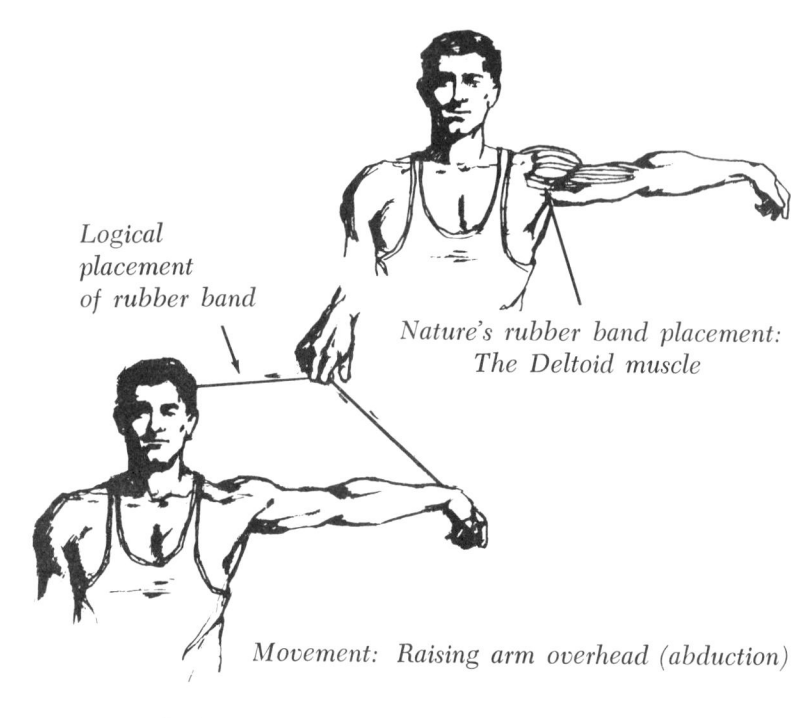

Nature's rubber band placement: The Deltoid muscle

Movement: Raising arm overhead (abduction)

FIGURE 40. *Recognizing a Primary Muscle*

SPECIFIC EXERCISES

On the assumption that you have begun your workouts as suggested in previous chapters (made a self-evaluation, and started flexibility and cardiovascular work), you should now be ready to choose from the following suggestions those ideas which fit your needs, desires, and time schedule.

The Best Sixteen

If you only have time for one exercise for each muscle area, the author considers the following sixteen exercises as the best for the particular primary muscle area on which they place stress. There is some overlap, but it is held to a minimum. These exercises are the best because they do isolate better than most, enabling you to build to the heavier weights with safety. On all of the exercises follow directions very carefully. In taking the bar from the floor keep in mind the simple rules for lifting any object: weight directly above the object (plus feet directly under the bar), knees bent, head up, and back firm and not bowed; unbend the knees to get the weight started from the floor.

FIGURE 41. *Two-Arm Press (Military Press)*

Primary Muscles: Deltoid (shoulder) and Triceps (posterior arm)
Directions: Overhand grip. Start with bar at clavicle, head up, back straight. Push directly overhead. Keep knees straight. Avoid *bending back during this press-up. Return slowly.*
Starting weight: 50-70 lbs.
Special caution: Avoid excessive leaning back. Keep eyes focused slightly upward.

#2—*Best Sixteen*

Two-Arm Curl. See Figure 36 for illustration.
Primary Muscles: Biceps brachii, Brachialis, and Brachioradialis.
Directions: Palms-up grip. Start with bar resting at thighs, elbows

straight and close to waist. Hands shoulder width apart. Keep upper arms still and bend elbows to raise the weight to touch the chest. Avoid bending the back during this elbow flexion. Keep elbows close to the body until almost finished, then allow them to move forward a little as your wrists curl slightly to bring the bar near the chest.

Starting Weight: 40-60 lbs.

Special Caution: "Cheat-Curls" do more harm than good. By hyper-extending your back to get a heavier weight curled you may damage your back. Perhaps even worse, you will not be working the primary muscles as much as when you do them correctly.

#3—Best Sixteen

Bent-Knee. Situps. See Figure 5 for illustration.

Primary Muscles: Rectus Abdominis, External Obliquus, Internal Obliquus, and Transversus Abdominis (Abdominal area).

Directions: Lie on back with hands clasped behind head and knees bent at 45° angle to the floor. Heels are almost flat. Slowly round back and bend head forward as you bring the upper trunk to a position at a 45° angle to the floor. Return to starting position. Feet may be stabilized at first. Later do it without this stabilization.

Starting Load: Do 5-10 repetitions, 2-3 sets.

Special Caution: The straight-legged situps are now out of date. They bring about an unusually high pressure on the lower back that can cause pain at a later time. Moreover, anatomists can clearly show that the abdominal muscles are not involved to as great a degree in the flexing of the trunk during the straight-legged situp.

Finally, using a weight to provide resistance can only serve to to hurt the lower back by promoting a hyper-extension. The strength which accrues is not great enough to warrant the potential danger.

Building Muscles

FIGURE 42. ½ Squats

Primary Muscles: Gluteus Maximus (Buttocks), Quadriceps (Front of Thigh), and Hamstrings (Back of Thigh).

Directions: Using spotters or a squat rack, get the bar rested across your shoulders, wide grip. Keeping the heels flat, bend very slowly until either your upper legs are parallel to the floor or you can no longer keep your heels flat. Keep head up and back straight.

Starting Weight: 50-75 lbs.

Special Caution: Do not raise heels—it destroys balance and limits the weight you can handle. Keep toes pointing straight ahead or only barely pointed outside to protect the medial ligaments of the knees.

FIGURE 43. *Heel Raises*

Primary Muscles: Gastrocnemius and Soleus (Calf area).
Directions: Get bar to shoulders as in ½ Squats. Simply raise up on your toes as fully as possible. Do repetitions in three toe positions: straight, angled out, and angled in. The board is for more advanced stages.
Starting Weight: 60-80 lbs.

Building Muscles 73

FIGURE 44. Straight-Legged Dead Lift

Primary Muscles: Erector Spinae and other muscles in immediate spinal cord area, Gluteus Maximus, and Hamstrings.
Directions: Place feet under bar. Keeping knees stiff and arms straight, straighten-up with the bar bringing it to thigh level. Allow shoulders to roll back slightly after straightening-up.
Starting Weight: 30-50 lbs.
Special Caution: Most people have not developed their backs well enough to do this exercise with much weight. Start low and build slowly.

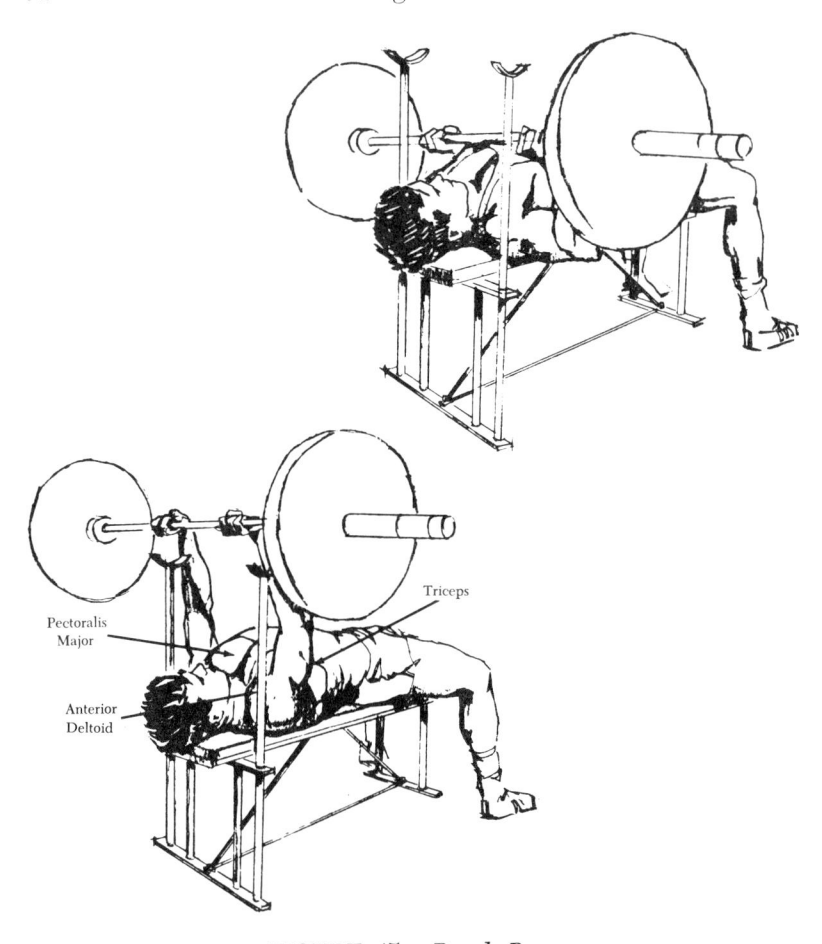

FIGURE 45. *Bench Press*

Primary Muscles: Anterior Deltoid, Pectoralis Major, and Triceps.
Directions: Lying flat on the bench, grip the bar with a palms-away grip wider than shoulder-width. Start from a straight-elbow position. Lower bar to chest and press back to the straight-elbow position. Keep buttocks on bench and back relatively flat during exercise.
Starting Weight: 50-75 lbs.
Special Caution: Use spotters as the weight increases. Again, do not damage your back by hyper-extending it just to impress someone with a heavy lift.

FIGURE 46. *Standing Lateral Raises*

Primary Muscles: Deltoid and Supraspinatus (shoulder area)

Directions: Simultaneously raise two dumbbells to an overhead position. Keep body erect and elbows straight. Grip with the palms toward you and arms in "attention" position.

Starting Weight: 5-10 lbs. each dumbbell.

76   Building Muscles

FIGURE 47. *Latissimus Dorsi Exercise*

Primary Muscles: Latissimus Dorsi (Large muscle covering back
Directions: Start in kneeling position below bar. Pull the bar dow
to the rear of the neck. Grip with palms-away wid
than shoulder-width.
Starting Weight: 40-70 lbs.
Special Caution: As weight increases you may be pulled from t
floor. A fixed seat and a belt must now be used.

Building Muscles 77

FIGURE 48. *Wrist Curls*

Primary Muscles: *Palms-up Grip—Wrist Flexors.*
Palms-down Grip—Wrist Extensors.
Directions: *Stabilize forearms on thighs. Move the weight slowly through full wrist joint range. Go directly up and down. Do not raise forearms from thighs.*
Starting Weight: *25-40 lbs.*

FIGURE 49. *Upright Rowing*

Primary Muscles: Deltoids (Shoulders), Trapezius (Neck) and Biceps Brachii.
Directions: Grip the bar with the palms-toward you and the hands close together. Keeping the back and legs straight, flex the elbows and raise the bar to the chin. Allow the elbows to come high (ear-level).
Starting Weight: 50-60 lbs.

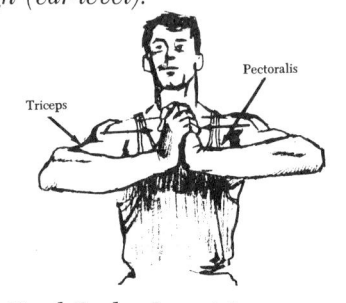

FIGURE 50. *Hand Push—Isometric*

Primary Muscles: Pectoralis (Chest) and Triceps (Posterior Arm)
Directions: Simply push palm against palm.
Starting Load: All Isometric Exercises, do 6 seconds at about effort, once a day. This need not vary nor progress

Building Muscles 79

FIGURE 51. *Prone Knee Flexion—Isometric*

Primary Muscles: Hamstrings (Back of Leg)
Directions: Lie on stomach with partner holding at ankle. (An immovable desk may be used, also.) Try to raise lower leg (Knee Flexion) from floor. Partner prevents raising.
Starting Load: 6 seconds each leg.

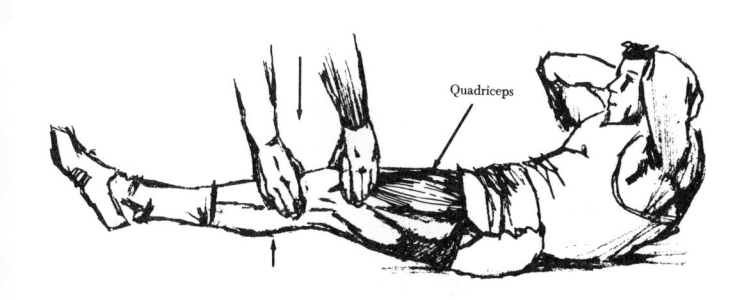

FIGURE 52. *Supine Leg Raise—Isometric*

Primary Muscles: Quadriceps (Front of Thigh).
Directions: Lie on back, head slightly raised, back rounded as much as possible. Partner holds at lower leg or knee and ankle. Try to raise entire leg in one piece. Partner prevents.
Starting Load: 6 seconds each leg.
Special Caution: Try not to hyperextend the back. Keep it somewhat rounded.

FIGURE 53. *Wall Push with Elbows—Isometric*

Primary Muscles: Posterior Deltoid (Rear Shoulder) and Rhomboids (Middle Back).
Directions: With back to a wall, arms out at shoulder level, and elbows bent, put pressure against the wall at the elbow rear arm area.
Starting Load: 6 seconds.

FIGURE 54. *Squeeze Rubber Ball*

Primary Muscles: Wrist Flexors and muscles of the hand.
Directions: Use a rubber ball the size of a tennis ball and squeeze it, relax, squeeze, relax, etc.
Starting Load: 15 per day with each hand.

Building Muscles 81

Suggestions For Variety

Some of the following exercises are excellent and could be used to provide variety in your workouts. They work many of the same muscle areas as the BEST SIXTEEN, but do so in slightly different ways:

Neck: Sternocleidomastoideus and Trapezius muscles primarily.

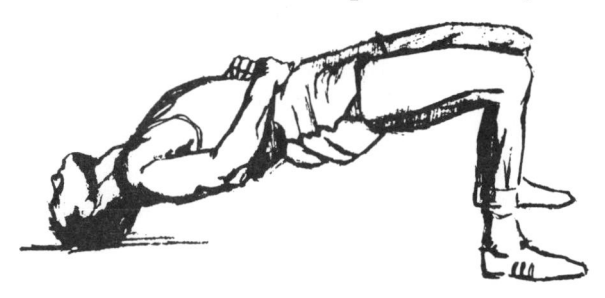

FIGURE 55. *Bridging (Neck Area)*

Balance and roll slowly *on head.*

FIGURE 56. *2-Man Set—Isometric (Neck Area)*

Head pulls in opposite direction

FIGURE 57. *Towel Pull—Isometric (Neck Area)*

FIGURE 58. *Neck Curls (Neck Area)*

Shoulders: Deltoid and Supraspinatus muscles primarily. Neck muscles, Rhomboids, Teres Major and Minor, and Latissimus Dorsi get work with many of these as well.

Roll shoulders slowly
Keep arms straight

FIGURE 59. *Shoulder Shrugs with Weight (Shoulder Area)*

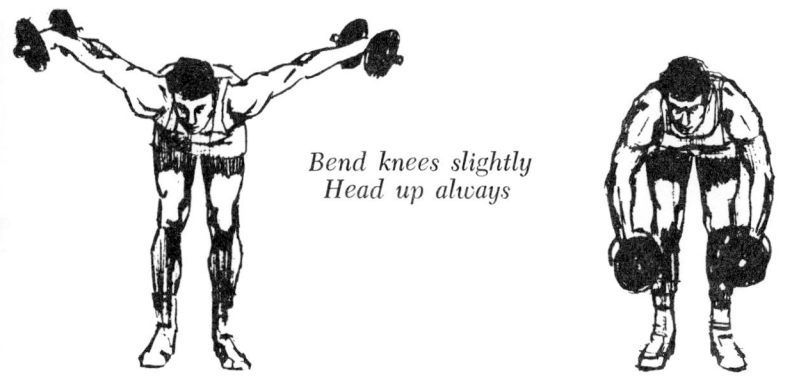

Bend knees slightly
Head up always

FIGURE 60. *Leaning Lateral Raise (Shoulder-Back Area)*

FIGURE 61. *Forward Raise*

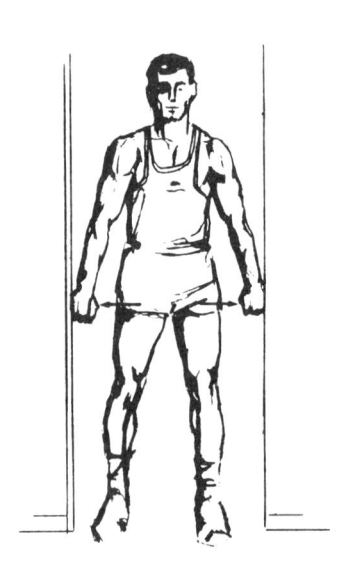

FIGURE 62. *Door Frame Lateral Raise—Isometric (Shoulder-Arm Area)*

Building Muscles

Back Of The Upper Arm: Triceps primarily. Shoulders and chest areas benefit from many of these exercises as well.

Pushups—See Figure 3, page 13.
Play catch with a medicine ball.

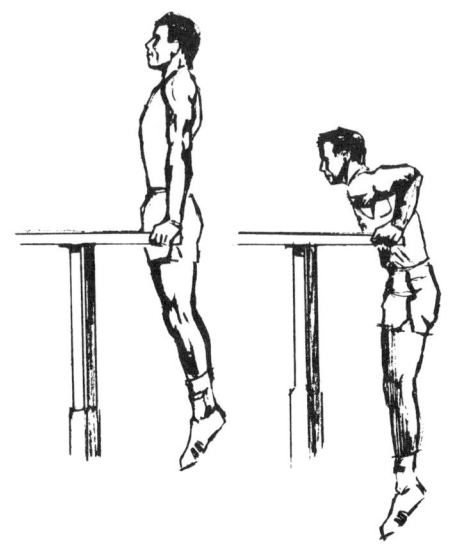

FIGURE 63. *Parallel Bar Dips (Triceps-Shoulder-Chest Area)*

FIGURE 64. *Behind the Neck Press (Triceps)*

Front Of The Arm: Biceps Brachii and flexing muscles of forearm primarily.

Chinups—See Figure 4, page 14.
Climbing the Rope.
Traveling the Ladder.

FIGURE 65. *Reverse Curls (Front of Entire Arm)*

*Keep elbow against
inside of knee throughout*

FIGURE 66. *Concentration Curl (Front of Arm)*

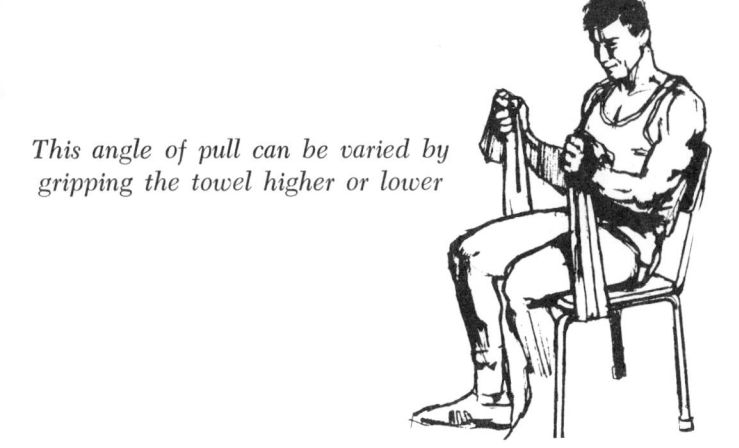

This angle of pull can be varied by gripping the towel higher or lower

FIGURE 67. *Towel Pull from Under Chair—Isometric (Front of Arm)*

Back: Primarily, the muscles that attach along the spinal cord, and the Latissimus Dorsi muscle. Gluteus muscles of the buttocks and the Hamstring muscles receive value from many of these, also.

Chinups, Leaning Lateral Raises, Ladder Traveling.

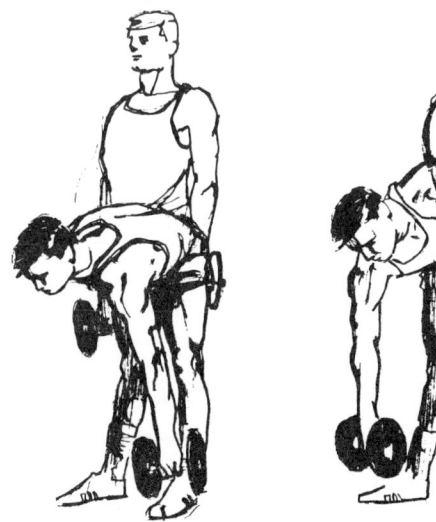

FIGURE 68. *Alternate Toe Touches with Dumbbells (Back Area)*

88   *Building Muscles*

FIGURE 69.   *Bent-Over Rowing (Back-Shoulder Area)*

Bring weight to chest area and return slowly in a slight oval. Be extremely careful with this exercise. Keep weights low to medium (25-65 lbs), never heavy.

FIGURE 70.   *Good Morning Exercise (Back Area)*

Abdominal Area:

FIGURE 71. *V-Ups (Abdominal Area)*

FIGURE 72. *Towel around Buttocks—Isometric (Middle of Trunk Area)*

Press buttocks back, pull towel forward, and tighten abdominal muscles.

FIGURE 73. *Side Bends with Dumbbells (Waist Area)*

Chest: Pectoralis Major and Minor primarily. The Latissimus Dorsi, Triceps, and the Anterior Deltoid get some benefit, also.

Pushups, Parallel Bar Dips.

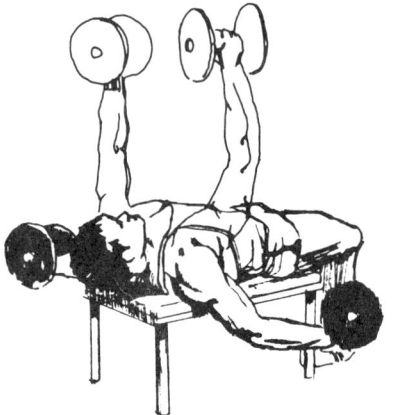

FIGURE 74. *Pectoralis Dumbbell Flies (Chest Area)*

Keep elbows slightly bent throughout exercise to prevent injury in elbow joint.

FIGURE 75. Fixed Bent Arm Pullovers (Latissimus Dorsi and Chest Area)

Keep lower back as flat to bench as possible.

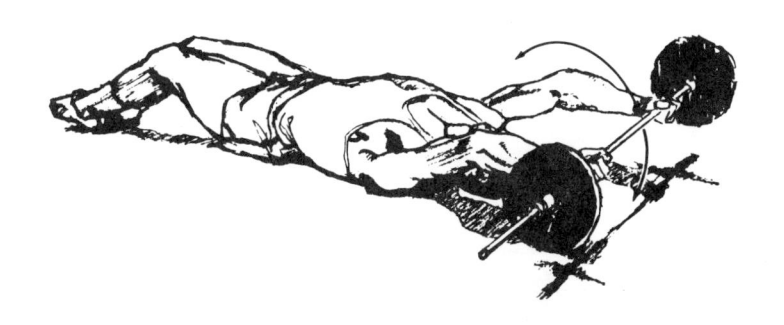

FIGURE 76. Straight Arm Pullovers (Latissimus Dorsi and Chest Area)

Keep knees slightly bent to eliminate as much as possible the hyperextending of the back.

Legs: Quadriceps, Hamstrings, Gastrocnemius, Soleus, Gluteus muscles.

FIGURE 77. *Squat Jumps with Barbells (Legs in General)*

FIGURE 78. *Knee Extensor with Iron Boot or Weighted Foot (Front of Thigh)*

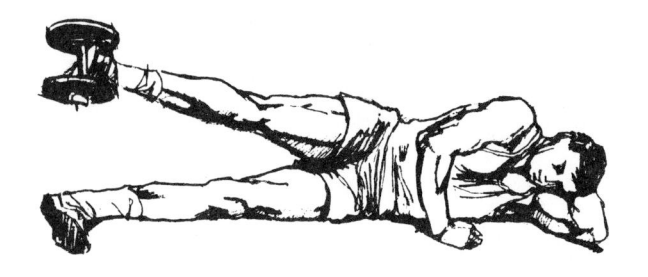

FIGURE 79. *Leg Abductor with Iron Boot (Lateral Leg Area)*

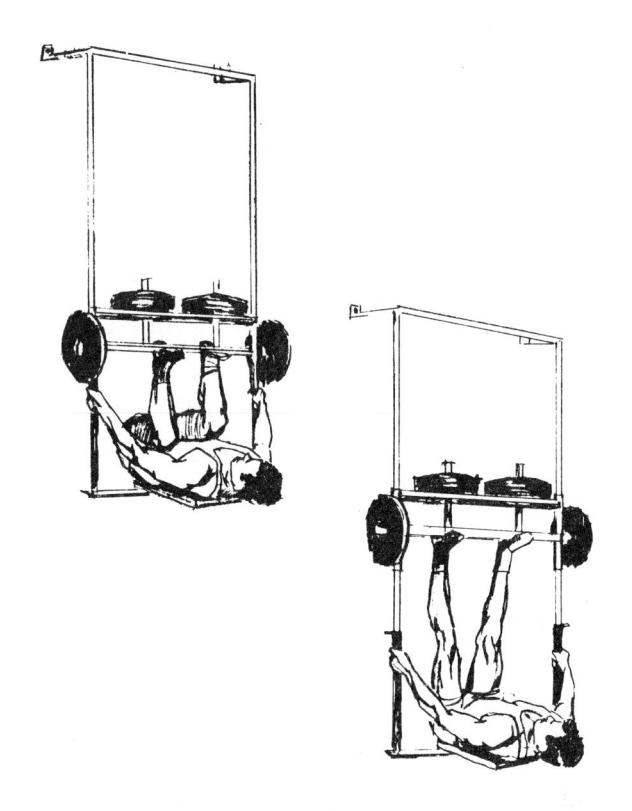

FIGURE 80. *Leg Presses—Machine (Legs in General)*

FIGURE 81. *Side-Straddle Hop with Weight (Legs in General)*

Power Exercises

The ideas for these five exercises came from the book by Hooks, *Application of Weight-Training to Athletics*,[4] and each demands that the performance be done according to directions. Otherwise, it may be possible to incur an injury.

FIGURE 82. *Knee Bend and Shoulder Press*

Primary Muscles: Quadriceps, Deltoids, and Triceps.
Directions: Place the barbell on shoulders, assume a shoulder-width grip, palms-up, and with the knees slightly bent. Thrust the bar directly overhead, straightening both elbows and knees. Return to shoulder position slowly.
Starting Weight: 40-70 lbs.

FIGURE 83. *High Pull-Up*

Primary Muscles: Quadriceps, Gluteus Maximus, Deltoids, and Biceps Brachii.
Directions: Weight is on the floor. Grasp with palms-down and on top of the bar. Hands are about six inches apart. Knees are bent, weight is directly below the knee. Standing quickly and straightening head and back, bring the weight to the chin in one motion. Keep elbows higher than hands throughout. You may jump slightly as you pull-up.
Starting Weight: 40-70 lbs.

FIGURE 84. *Power Press*

Primary Muscles: Quadriceps, Deltoids, and Triceps.
Directions: Do the same as the Two-Hand Press, FIGURE 41, but bend knees at start and thrust the bar rather than slowly pressing it up.
Starting Weight: 60-85 lbs.
Special Caution: As in the Two-Hand Press, avoid hyperextending the back.

FIGURE 85. *Power Curl*

Primary Muscles: Quadriceps, Gluteus Maximus, and Biceps Brachii.
Directions: Start in a crouched position with curl-grip. Come quickly to a standing position while curling the bar to the collarbone area. Return bar to floor in same arc at a fairly rapid rate.
Starting Weight: 50-70 lbs.
Special Caution: Keep head and shoulders back to avoid back strain, but do not hyper-extend back.

FIGURE 86. *Modified Clean*

Primary Muscles: Quadriceps, Gluteus Maximus, Deltoids, and Biceps Brachii.
Directions: In crouched position, over-hand grip, head up, and back straight. Start the lift by using legs and hips. As they straighten, begin pulling the bar up in front of you and rise on toes. As the bar reaches shoulder level, dip under it, and bring it to rest at the chest. Thrust the elbows and wrists under the bar quickly during this last movement. This should all be one continuous movement. Now straighten the body. Return bar to floor. Be sure to bend the knees as you do.
Starting Weight: 50-75 lbs.

Warning

The instructions for each exercise are explicit; follow them *exactly*. The proper form can eliminate major injuries as well as the small aches and pains that sometimes accompany weight-training. Equally as important is that proper form will prevent the loss of range of motion. A myth perpetrated about weight-training postulates that lifting weights causes one to become *muscle-bound*. This *can* happen if the lifter fails to flex and extend to the greatest degree possible. Note Figure 87 for correct and incorrect executions. By correctly lifting and lowering through the full range of motion the conditioner stands little chance of losing any functional flexibility. As a matter of fact, he should gain some. One exception to this rule has been taken in terms of the SQUATS exercise. This has resulted from the unique structure of the knee and the fact that most people have weakened that structure in some way before beginning weight-training. This is not the case in the other joints of the body.

The Incorrect Way   *The Correct Way*

FIGURE 87. *Avoiding Muscle-boundedness*

Isometric exercises may bring on a loss of range in motion if they are the only types of exercise used. For that reason it is advised that you follow an isometric exercise with an isotonic exercise for the same muscle area. It would be best to use a relatively light weight, perhaps one enabling you to make ten to twelve repetitions. If weights are not available, simply move the limb through the full range of motion several times after completing the isometric contraction.

Breathing

Great stress is placed by some lifters on proper breathing during lifting. The research is not in agreement at this time about the values of the different techniques. But one thing is apparent; DO NOT HOLD YOUR BREATH WHILE EXERCISING. The pressure builds in the thoracic cavity. The blood pressure rises reducing the return of venous blood to the right side of the heart (the Valsalva Phenomenon). It is vital to reduce this pressure by exhaling as the weight reaches its peak.

The general rule followed in most exercises is to inhale quickly, not excessively, at the start of muscle contraction. As the weight is lifted, slowly begin to let the air escape. Upon lowering the weight breathe in briefly just as it starts down and breathe out slowly as the weight gets back to the starting position. NEVER BREATHE TOO HEAVILY. The combined effect of a deep inspiration and the Valsalva Phenomenon could induce a "blackout." Short "gulps" would be best for the inspiration phase. Blow the air out steadily as the weight reaches the peak points. There is no need to hold the breath during isometric work, either. Let a little air escape by leaving the mouth open during the exercise.

References

1. T. Hettinger, *Physiology of Strength* (Springfield, Illinois: Charles C Thomas, Publisher, 1961), p. 75.
2. H. II. Clarke and D. Glines, "Relationships of Reaction, Movement, and Completion Times to Motor, Strength, Anthropometric, and Maturity Measures of 13-Year-Old Boys," *Research Quarterly*, Vol. 33 (May, 1962) 201.
3. V. DiGiovanna, "The Relation of Selected Structural and Functional Measures to Success in College Athletics," *Research Quarterly*, Vol. 14 (May, 1943) 213.
4. G. Hooks, *Application of Weight Training to Athletics* (Englewood Cliffs, N.J.: Prentice-Hall, Inc., 1962), pp. 69-74.

7

Tying It All Together

Summary Of Important Concepts

This book has attempted to deal with the concept, physical fitness, as it affects the total life of an individual. The key rationale proposed for engaging in a vigorous physical conditioning program has been psychological. Evidence has been cited to impress upon you that *happiness*, effective living, a positive self-concept, or whatever the ingredients are in the so-called "good life," can be achieved best through an integrated organism. Disintegration occurs to the degree that each individual disunites his physical functions from his mental and emotional reactions.

The existence of certain physiological fundamentals has been suggested. *Facts* have been offered about the manner in which the body functions. Physical fitness has been broken down into several components and approaches to optimal development of each component have been submitted. You have been urged to analyze your own needs and desires, weigh them relative to the fundamental laws governing body processes, and then choose the method of conditioning that most interests you.

A program designed for general physical fitness has been suggested as the wisest approach for the average person. The concept that the body is a *total organism* with no single function of it ever working alone begets such advice. If any one component is neglected it subtracts from all others in almost every situation. With these ideas as a foundation the following outline is offered as an integration of the information presented in the earlier chapters.

Outline Of A General Conditioning Program (GCP)

I. Spend about 1½ weeks loosening up before trying anything strenuous.
   A. Work 15-30 minutes every other day on "Warm-up and Flexibility" exercises as suggested in Chapters Two and Four.
   B. Jog slowly every day for about 2-5 minutes.

II. Take the Fitness Tests suggested in Chapter Two.

III. Begin a 30-45 minute program every other day similar to the following:
   A. Loosen up with 4-5 flexibility exercises, Chapter Four.
   B. Jog slowly for about 5 minutes.
   C. Alternate one set of each "Best Sixteen" exercises with 10-30 seconds of a flexibility exercise, and 10-30 seconds of complete rest.
   D. Finish with a swim, or if you have time, play your favorite vigorous sport for about another one-half an hour. (Your skill may suffer at first from the weight training, so you may want to start the day by playing the sport.)

IV. After several months, try the following 60-minute program for every day:
   A. Monday, Wednesday, and Friday:
      1. Loosen up with your favorite 4-5 flexibility exercises.
      2. Do 2-3 sets of your favorite muscle-building exercises suggested in Chapter Six. This will probably mean no more than 20 if some are isometric, or no more than 12 if all are weight-lifting exercises.
      3. Finish with a swim, or your favorite vigorous sport.
   B. Tuesday, Thursday, and Saturday:
      1. Loosen up with about 10 flexibility exercises.
      2. Jog slowly for one-half mile.
      3. Walk about 5 minutes.
      4. Begin your Interval Running Program as suggested in Chapter Five.
   C. Sunday: Take a walk and relax.

SPECIAL IDEAS

For The Athlete

The GCP would be an excellent one, even for the highly-specialized athlete, assuming that each reader will choose weight training exercises and running programs that fit his or her special interests. However, certain activities may be tried by the athlete beyond the GCP to benefit an individual sports skill.

Many myths abound regarding the developing and retaining of highly productive and aesthetic athletic skills. Many coaches have shied away from any programs other than running for their athletes. In recent years the trend has been changed somewhat. When it was learned, for example, that the great Ted Williams used weights, baseball coaches began to look into the various programs. The University of Iowa basketball teams in the 1950's proved that weight-training was of great benefit to basketball skills. The unusual strength of Wilt Chamberlain has added to the desire for more strength to promote basketball prowess. In football the attempt has been made to build strength through isometric as well as weight training programs. The professional teams use these ideas extensively, but the most value can be realized with younger, growing boys.[1] The prevention of injuries would be reason enough to strengthen the muscles and tendons around the knees, ankles, elbows, and shoulders. But as has been pointed out in earlier chapters, skill is heightened by increased strength.

The creativeness of an experienced weight-trainer and isometric conditioner will help in designing several exercises involving the skills for each sport. After several months of conditioning, you should have that kind of sophistication. Simply imagine the skill and employ a resistance to it. Several good books are available which deal with conditioning for specific sports. Hooks' *Application of Weight Training to Athletics*[2] is one of the best. However, the following outline should give you a brief idea of several possible approaches.

Baseball: The muscles of the shoulders, the arms, and the hands need special treatment for this sport. Such exercises as these are excellent:

Tying It All Together

1. Forward and Lateral Raises from erect or leaning positions.
2. Dynamic shoulder exercises such as chinups, rope climbing, and Parallel Bar Dips.
3. The Two-Arm Press and the Bench Press.
4. Wrist Curls, Rope-Winding, squeezing of a rubber ball, and wrist work with dumbbell loaded on one end only.
5. Finger-tip Pushups.
6. Isometric exercises involving the wrist. Hold on the fingers at sides or on top.
7. Stiff-Legged Dead-Lift.
8. Exercises involving bat or ball. (See Hooks' *Weight Training Applied to Athletics*, pp. 124–127).

Basketball: The legs are vital, of course, but strong hands and shoulders mean a lot of rebounds and three-point plays. The following exercises should be emphasized:

1. Half Squats.
2. Heel Raisers.
3. Power Squat Jump and Side Straddle Hop with weight.
4. Same exercises for the upper body and back as for the baseball player.
5. Two-Arm Curl.
6. Upright-Rowing.
7. See Hooks' *Weight Training Applied to Athletics*, pp. 142–147 for some excellent ideas involving basketball equipment.

Football: There is no joint in the extremities that is safe in football, if it is under-strengthened. But special emphasis usually should be placed in strengthening the neck and the knee. Therefore, beyond the GCP, extra sets of the following exercises should be tried:

1. Neck bridging and the Two Man Set Isometric.
2. Upright Rowing.
3. Half Squats.
4. Heel Raisers.
5. Leg Press Machine.
6. Boot Raises.
7. Prone Knee Bending Isometric.

More ideas relative to these and other sports are available, but if the GCP is followed and the exercises mentioned here are emphasized, almost all strength needs can be met. Such sports as tennis, track, golf, and handball require much this same sort of approach: an analysis of the specific muscle areas most used and/or most susceptible to injury. With a little creativity and the knowledge you now have about exercise programs it should not be difficult to design a specialized program.

One caution should be offered about weight-training during the season. Unless your strength is greatly below normal functioning it would be wise to curtail the weight-training at this time. Running programs and isometric exercising can and should be continued with some adjustments for game days.

Finally, athletes are notorious for their off-season and retirement exercise habits. In many cases they continue to eat as heavily as they did during the peak of the season, or their careers. But since their activity has decidedly lessened, they begin to get fat. Sometimes this brings about coronary problems in the late thirties or in the forties. This has led to the myth of *the athlete's heart*. People conclude that athletes die young *because* of their active lives. Doctors tell us that people who constantly allow their weight to fluctuate are more prone to heart disease than others. That some athletes engage in this practice throughout their careers and then settle into a steady obesity upon retirement cannot be denied. There is a pattern established of robust playing and eating, then complete relaxation and/or dissipation. It is this pattern that causes the heart problem, not the active life.

In actuality, the athlete should live longer than most people. All of his youth and early adulthood are spent usually in building a strong large heart and a sturdy muscular system. These are positive health attributes, which if maintained to some reasonable degree, cannot help but aid in the happy and effective living of middle and old-age.

The large, healthy heart does not cause the heart attacks. Like any other muscle the undiseased heart grows bigger and more functional with use, exercise. It is only when the athlete stops playing, but continues to eat heavily that his well-developed heart suffers. Fatty tissue begins to surround it, the fibers grow weaker and smaller, and the functioning of the entire body suffers. His heart trouble stems from the accumulation of fat about a once-large heart, not from the fact that he was once an athlete.

The heart that is defective or diseased is a problem completely alien to the point being made here. This is a condition not associated with activity in any way whatsoever.

Obesity, Exercise, And Diet

It is a sad fact, but many people never associate these three items. So often the obese young man or woman will start on a conditioning program hoping to lose weight without recognizing the need to begin a program of dieting at the same time. Exercise is marvelous; it can burn up calories; it can even reduce the appetite after a long enough time. *But exercise needs help.*

Due to a decrease in certain metabolic actions after the age of twenty, a person gains about one pound a year. This metabolic slowdown continues with age due to decreased exercise, lessened muscle tonus, and diminishing activity by certain of the ductless glands, especially the sex glands and the thyroid. This is a natural occurrence with which many people fail to reckon. They continue their same eating and exercise habits as when they were twenty and cannot understand the weight gain. As you can see, by the time they are forty they will be twenty pounds overweight.

Many detractors of exercise say that it is worthless. After all, to lose one pound of fat a man must walk thirty-six hours, or split wood for seven hours, or play volleyball for eleven hours. And who is going to do that? No one—*at one stretch*—but if the wood-chopping or the walking are spread out in one-half hour a day blocks, the task of losing a pound is not nearly so imposing. One-half hour of handball or squash per day would be equivalent to sixteen pounds a year.

Of course, this reasoning is designed to promote regular, sensible exercise habits. But you might say: "After a half an hour of handball I'm ready to eat a horse, won't I gain more weight as a result?" No, according to studies by Mayer of Harvard that have been done on animals and humans. It was discovered that persons engaged in regular, continuing strenuous activity actually reduced their food intake relative to what it was prior to exercise. Moreover, it was found that subjects who were inactive increased their calorie intake over the same period.[3] These are significant studies because they indicate that obesity follows from a lack of exercise rather than preceding it. So the fat get fatter and the thin get thinner. Why won't people do something about it? As you have seen, apathy or passiveness can be dangerous because of the natural metabolic slowdown. Something positive must be done or death may be the result.

Is death too strong a word? Science has shown an enormously significant correlation between obesity and functional diseases of the heart, circulatory system, kidneys, and pancreas. Insurance companies almost double their rates for the obese knowing that fat people have a poorer chance of recovery from operations and serious illnesses than do other people. That there are other disadvantages to being fat like difficulty in getting about, disfigurement, mental and physical sluggishness, are also reasons for positive action.

The average person leading a moderately active life needs about fifteen calories per pound a day to maintain his present weight. Thus a 150 pound man would need no more than 2250 calories each day to remain at 150 pounds. Each pound of stored fat contains 3500 to 400 calories. In order to lose one pound a week through dieting it is necessary to consume 500-600 calories less than the figure calculated at 1 times present weight, which is the kind of diet recommended by most doctors. If the diet is combined with an exercise program, it can (after a period of time) be adjusted to with ease. Without the exercise may be that the 500 less calories per day will seem as vital a loss as oxygen. Most of us do not have the will power to do it, so let exercise help.

It would be wrong to make such a program sound too simple. Other tactics are necessary. The types of food you ingest must be consideration. Carbohydrates are known to be oxidized preferentially for muscular energy. They yield more calories per liter of oxygen than any other type of food. In short, they are efficient. During exercise one needs to use his oxygen wisely as you have learned in previous chapters. It is for this reason that carbohydrates are highly recommended to anyone about to embark on a strenuous task.

However, when the carbohydrates are not used in energy production, they lend themselves to the production of fat. For this reason carbohydrate intake must be wisely regulated by exercise habits as well as basic bodily needs. The nutritionist, Bogert, suggests in very strong terms that sugars and sweets should furnish no more than 8-1 percent of the total calorie intake of the average sedentary person. The person who engages in strenuous labor and/or is of great physical size may exceed this level, but there is seldom any need to go beyond 15-17 percent of the total calorie intake.

The following diet is suggested as a foundation to guide the average adult:[5]

1. Milk—1 pint daily.
2. Meats—1 serving (3½ ounces of the cooked, edible portion).
3. 1 egg—not necessarily every day, but at least 3-4 per week.
4. 1 serving of another protein food (50 grams) like extra milk, egg, cheese, legumes, or nuts.
5. Vegetables: 1 potato, 1 average serving (100 grams) of leafy green or yellow vegetables, and 1 average serving any other type vegetable.
6. Fruits: 1 average serving citrus fruit, tomato, or other rich source of vitamin C.
7. 2 tablespoons of butter or fortified margarine.
8. Bread and/or cereal: 4 slices of whole grain or enriched bread.

There is nothing too painful in these diet suggestions; most of the good things can be tasted with it. Moderation appears to be the key. If time, money, or the nature of your present vocation make these basic standards difficult to meet, Bogert suggests some excellent ways to substitute intelligently. There really is no substitute for milk and the adult who deludes himself on this point may run into trouble.

However, where a potato is unavailable, corn, peas, or beans may supply the nutritive elements needed. Moreover, weight balance may be maintained by cutting out the potato at a meal where another starchy vegetable like corn is served.

Some fruits may be substituted for the yellow vegetables, but the leafy greens are irreplaceable as a source for vitamin A, iron, B-complex of vitamins, vitamin C, or calcium.[6]

Fats should make up no more than 20 percent of the total calories in a diet, but they should be a part of the diet for their vitamin A value as well as their role in being a reserve energy source. Where a fresh fruit may provide the nutrition that a pie formerly supplied, such a substitution is recommended; however, a crash diet with no fats may be extremely dangerous. When confronted with these kinds of decisions it would be best to consult a qualified doctor or a nutritionist.

Proteins are tremendously essential, but as recent studies have shown, a diet of excess protein intake is unnecessary,[7] and in the case of strenuous exercise it is less effective than a high carbohydrate meal. One researcher suggests that a rich carbohydrate meal (say spaghetti) would be far better for an athlete as a pre-game meal than a high protein meal.[8] The reason is that carbohydrates burn more efficiently than fats and proteins; in fact, proteins contribute little or nothing to the production of energy, their role is in muscle mass increase, not muscle movement. A second factor is that proteins are a source of fixed acids that can only be eliminated by urinary excretion. During a game or strenuous workout such a discomfort would not be welcome. For these reasons it is rather silly to take protein supplements. The normal intake will produce the same results and in many cases more healthful ones. This is not to say that the amount of protein one eats should not increase as he trains with weights or runs, but the increase is commensurate with the rest of his diet and his new calorie out-flow.

It may be interesting also to note that three meals per day is no longer considered sacred. Some researchers have found that five meals per day, smaller at each sitting but equal in total calorie intake to the three meal sittings, lead to a greater work output.[9] The elimination of breakfast was found to cause very significant decreases in work output.[10] These kinds of research have implication for the person "on the go." The idea of eating less, but more often, may fit the schedule of a busy person much better than the production that is now a part of our mealtime pattern. Even a small but nutritious breakfast can supply energy sources for many hours. Of course, the problem is that many people who are big eaters will find it difficult to reduce the calorie intake at each meal. As a result, they are liable to end up eating many more calories than needed.

So the problem is not a simple one. Science can provide some hints—no crash diets, exercise daily, eat a balanced diet, substitute intelligently—but it would seem that it all narrows down to the application of this knowledge by a determined and intelligent individual. The individual who deludes himself that these ingredients of "will power" and "thinking-power" are not vital to his approach to losing weight is in for disappointment.

For one thing, he becomes easy prey for quack schemes relative to exercise. One present-day ruse is the idea that one can take off weight in a particular body area *before* reducing the total body weight. Such things as massaging the buttocks or abdominal area have become popular based on this delusion.

All of us store our fat in places peculiar to our own body. For many people these areas are the waistline and the chin. Exercises can improve the muscle tone, the circulation, and the strength in these areas, but if the calorie intake exceeds the calorie use, the accumulation of fat will continue in these same "personal reservoirs." Massage can only increase the flow of blood to an area, but it will have no effect on the fatty tissue which resides there. This tissue will not "flow-off" with the blood.

As a result, the only approach to reducing the waistline is a general one involving exercise and diet. The General Conditioning Program is highly recommended with the following variations for the fat man:

1. Admit right now that you have a disease as demanding of regular care as diabetes. With this recognition it should be easier to devote a small part of *every* day to exercise and the forming of every meal around a calorie-count.
2. Work into the GCP slowly until your weight is within 10-15 pounds of normal. This will require anywhere from a month to a year of sensible dieting depending upon the amount of overweight present.
3. Emphasize flexibility and exercises for local-muscle-endurance until within 10-15 pounds of normal. The running should be very moderate and never overloaded until this time. The following suggestions might be followed:
   a. Do Stiff-Legged Dead Lifts with a light weight—perhaps 15-25 repetitions rapidly.
   b. Use light dumbbells to do Alternate Toe Touches With Weight. Try to do 15-25 repetitions.
   c. Do 3 sets of Bent-Knee Situps in this order:
      1) 5-25 normally (25 after you have conditioned awhile).
      2) 5-25 from three angles. As you come down each time, angle your body to first the right, then situp, come down to the left, situp, and then come down straight.
      3) Do 10 situps with a 2-second hold at the position of a 45° angle to the floor.
   d. Do side bends with one dumbbell at a time. Try 2-3 sets of 10 repetitions to each side.

The more vigorous program definitely should be started when the weight has been reduced to within 10-15 pounds of normal.

Remember that weight training and isometrics build muscles a does most conditioning. Weight may be gained from an overload situation. Thus, if heavy weight-training is avoided at first and the dieting is practiced strictly, a loss of fatty tissue should result. After a while muscle tissue will account for increased weight that is now attributable to fat, which is the goal. Do not worry about numbers of pound gained or lost; rather, keep a "grabbing-count," of the fatty deposit around your stomach, back, posterior arm, or wherever it may be stored on you. This loose measure should provide more satisfactio than the daily scale readings.

The amount of fluid in the body fluctuates a great deal; on som people, water-weight can vary as much as ten pounds in one day Steam baths reduce the water content of the body, but not the fatt tissue. For this reason, they are highly over-rated as a reduction too After a steam bath you should be thirsty. Go ahead and drink. You body is not only begging for it, it *needs* the liquid. Of course, now what has happened? Your weight goes back up. The alternative coul be dangerous. If the body is denied the water, the core temperatur rises dramatically. The same sort of thing can happen if one uses rubber suit on a humid day to reduce weight. In the case of the rub ber suit the body is denied the chance to sweat freely. Again, the cor temperature rises dangerously. The balance of salt to water must b maintained within the organism. If it is not, a heat stroke and pos sible death can be the result.

There is no easy solution. Massage, steam baths, and rubber sui are all approaches used by people looking for the end of the rainbov The fat man must work hard to achieve his goal, it is a dangerou delusion to believe otherwise.

The Underweight Problem

The underweight person, usually an ectomorph, does not have th urgent need to take special, lifetime measures like the fat man. Bu the problem in being underweight is that it can usually be correlate with poor functioning, respiratory disorders, and a sense of weakne damaging to the self-image.

Weight-training and diet can perform wonders in relieving thes problems. Again, special diets are not necessary. Simply expandir

Tying It All Together

normal, balanced meal sensibly can produce the framework on which exercise can build. Three meals a day are traditional and therefore may be easy to develop into a habit. This is the initial step which the underweight person must take. Begin eating regularly. Having only coffee and a doughnut for breakfast will destroy all the good that one may do the rest of the day. It is imperative to get a good breakfast and a sound mid-day meal. The evening meal is important, but since rest usually follows it, there is less urgency about it than the other two. This kind of reasoning is often reversed much to the detriment of the person trying to gain weight.

There is no great need to take extra proteins or vitamins. If a doctor recommends a specific supplement based on a thorough examination of your metabolism, then go ahead. But willy-nilly taking of protein or vitamin supplements is a waste of money and can be damaging to the system. The body needs just so many vitamins and proteins per day; too few cause nutritional-deficiency diseases like Ricketts or Beri-Beri; too many are eliminated as waste products (however, some excess vitamins have been known to cause bone damage). In this country Ricketts and Beri-Beri are almost non-existent due to the wide variety of foods available. It is almost impossible for the average eater to be vitamin or protein-deficient. And since an excess is not used by the body, it is not too difficult to conclude that supplements are not needed.

Just as with the fat man, the process of weight-control is slow and challenging; there are no quick answers. But by following Bogert's suggestions for a foundation diet, it should be possible to gain bulk and muscle-weight within two months after beginning an exercise program. The food intake should be increased at the same rate as the exercise level.

The General Conditioning Program is as good a starting program as any for the exercise portion of the task. Make the following adjustments to maximize the results:

1. Work only every other day; on the off-day relax completely. Give your system a chance to recover.
2. Reduce the running program to slow jogging. Just try to run in a relaxed manner for longer and longer periods of time. Once your weight has risen to normal, and if you desire, start the Interval Running Program.

3. After the first few weeks of orienting yourself to the conditioning program, use just the following exercises with the sets and repetitions as suggested:
   a. Two-Arm Press: 4-5 sets, 10-8-6-4-2 repetitions. Remember that the weight used is always heavy enough that you can barely make the last repetition.
   b. Do slow Bent-Knee Situps between sets of the Two-Arm Press. Do only 10 situps each time and do slowly. Then rest until ready for the next set of the Two-Arm Press.
   c. One-Half Squats: 3 sets, 15-12-10 repetitions.
   d. Alternate Wrist Curls with One-Half Squats: Do 3 sets at 10 repetitions.
   e. Two-Arm Curl: same as Two-Arm Press for sets and repetitions.
   f. Alternate the Curl with 2-Man Set neck isometric: 6-second hold. If no partner, do Towel Pull isometric for neck.
   g. Heel Raisers: Same sets and repetitions as Squat.
   h. Alternate with Shoulder Shrugs With Weight: Do 3 sets at 10 repetitions.
   i. Bench Press: 5 sets, 10-8-6-4-2 repetitions.
   j. Alternate with Slow Dead Lift: 3 sets, all at 10 repetitions. Rest between the last two Bench Press sets.

If more time is available, which is doubtful, such exercises as these help to build bulk: Bent Arm Pullover, Parallel Bar Dips, Chinup, Latissimus Dorsi Bar Exercise, and Pectoralis Flies.

The term "normal weight" has been used quite often. This is an extremely nebulous term, but the following weight charts should give you as close an approximation as is possible at the present time. Chapter Two you were instructed in the technique of discerning your somatotype. These charts of representative somatotypes should aid you in estimating your normal weight. The comments with each chart are paraphrased from Dr. Sheldon's classic book on the subject, *Atlas of Men*.

That you have read to this point is a most hopeful sign. If you have acted upon what you have read, then you are ready for the joys and the challenges of the only real "good life" possible, the "active life."

Keep moving.

Tying It All Together

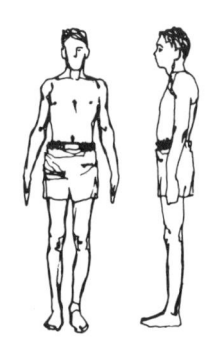

FIGURE 88. Somatotype 117

Description: The "Walking Stick." Extreme Ectomorph. Very rare. Classic "egghead" of the college campus.

Weight for Age and Height

Height (inches)	18	23	28	33	38	43	48	53	58
75	130	130	130	131	131	131	132	131	..
74	125	125	125	126	126	126	127	126	..
73	120	120	120	121	121	121	122	121	..
72	115	115	115	116	116	116	117	116	..
71	111	111	111	112	112	112	112	111	..
70	106	106	106	107	107	107	108	108	..
69	102	102	102	103	103	103	103	102	..
68	98	98	98	99	99	99	99	98	..
67	93	93	94	94	94	94	94	93	..
66	89	89	89	90	90	90	90	90	..
65	85	85	85	86	86	86	86	85	..
64	81	81	82	82	82	82	82	81	..
63	77	77	77	78	78	78	78	78	..
62	74	74	74	75	75	75	75	74	..
61	70	70	70	71	71	71	71	71	..

The weight charts and comments which appear in FIGURES 89-98 are reprinted from William Sheldon, *Atlas of Men* (New York: Harper & Row, Publishers, 1954). This chart is from p. 366.

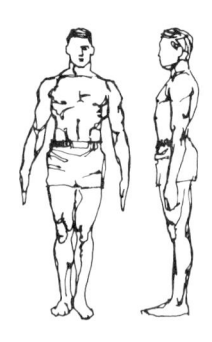

FIGURE 89. *Somatotype 171*

Description: Extreme Mesomorph. Maximal human muscularity. Takes on weight in affluent America. Welcomes strenuous life.

Weight for Age and Height

Height (inches)	18	23	28	33	Age 38	43	48	53	58	63
75	218	220	223	228	232	233	236	234	233	233
74	208	212	214	218	222	224	226	225	224	224
73	200	203	206	209	213	215	217	215	215	215
72	192	195	198	201	205	207	209	208	207	207
71	184	187	190	193	197	199	200	199	198	198
70	177	180	182	186	189	191	192	191	190	190
69	169	173	175	178	181	183	184	183	182	182
68	162	165	168	170	173	175	176	175	174	174
67	155	158	160	163	165	168	168	168	167	167
66	148	151	153	156	158	160	161	160	159	159
65	141	144	146	149	151	153	154	153	152	152
64	135	137	139	142	144	146	147	146	145	145
63	129	131	133	135	137	139	140	139	138	138
62	122	125	127	129	131	133	133	133	132	132
61	117	119	121	123	124	126	127	126	125	125

Atlas of Men, p. 64.

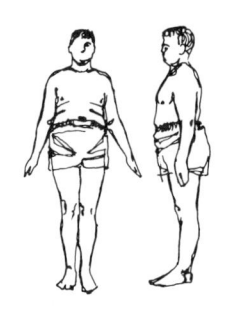

FIGURE 90. *Somatype 711*

Description: Extreme Endormorph. Doubt if one exists. Often has difficulty competing in the American culture.

Weight for Age and Height

Height (inches)	18	23	28	33	Age 38	43	48	53	58	63
75	281	316	352	383	365	..	..	..	..	..
74	270	302	338	367	350	..	..	..	..	..
73	259	289	325	353	336	..	..	..	..	..
72	249	278	311	339	322	..	..	..	..	..
71	238	267	298	326	309	..	..	..	..	..
70	228	256	286	312	296	..	..	..	..	..
69	219	245	274	298	280	..	..	..	..	..
68	209	235	262	285	273	..	..	..	..	..
67	200	225	250	272	260	..	..	..	..	..
66	191	215	239	259	247	..	..	..	..	..
65	182	205	228	248	236	..	..	..	..	..
64	174	196	218	236	226	..	..	..	..	..
63	166	187	208	225	215	..	..	..	..	..
62	158	178	199	215	205	..	..	..	..	..
61	151	170	189	206	196	..	..	..	..	..

las of Men, p. 324.

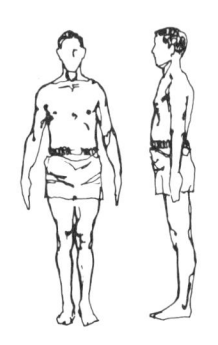

FIGURE 91. Somatotype 244

Description: Balanced
Mesomorph-Ectomorph.
4 percent of the male
population. The wiry
and slender young man.
Common on advertising
magazines. Likely to
be long-lived.

Weight for Age and Height

Height (inches)	18	23	28	33	38	43	48	53	58	63
75	170	175	179	181	184	186	188	189	190	191
74	163	168	172	174	177	178	180	181	182	182
73	157	162	165	168	170	171	173	174	175	176
72	150	155	158	160	163	164	166	167	168	168
71	144	148	152	154	156	157	159	160	161	161
70	138	142	146	148	150	151	153	154	155	155
69	132	137	140	142	144	145	147	147	148	149
68	127	131	134	135	138	139	140	141	142	142
67	121	125	128	129	132	132	134	135	136	136
66	115	119	122	124	126	126	128	129	129	130
65	110	114	116	118	120	121	122	123	124	124
64	105	109	111	113	115	115	117	117	118	118
63	100	104	106	108	109	110	111	112	113	113
62	96	99	101	103	104	105	106	106	108	108
61	91	94	96	98	99	100	101	101	102	102

Atlas of Men, p. 93.

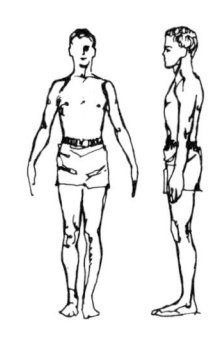

FIGURE 92. *Somatotype 335*

Description: Commonest Ectomorph. Usually tall. Posture seldom pleases physical educators.

Weight for Age and Height

Height (inches)	18	23	28	33	38	Age 43	48	53	58	63
75	164	169	173	177	179	181	183	183	183	183
74	158	162	166	169	172	174	176	176	176	176
73	152	156	160	163	165	167	169	169	169	169
72	146	150	153	157	159	161	163	163	163	163
71	139	143	146	150	152	153	155	155	155	155
70	133	137	140	143	146	147	149	149	149	149
69	128	131	135	137	140	141	143	143	143	143
68	122	126	129	132	134	135	137	137	137	137
67	117	120	123	126	128	129	131	131	131	131
66	112	115	117	120	122	123	125	125	125	125
65	107	109	112	114	116	118	119	119	119	119
64	102	104	107	109	111	112	114	114	114	114
63	97	100	102	104	106	107	109	109	109	109
62	93	95	98	99	101	102	103	103	103	103
61	88	90	93	95	96	97	99	99	99	99

Atlas of Men, p. 147.

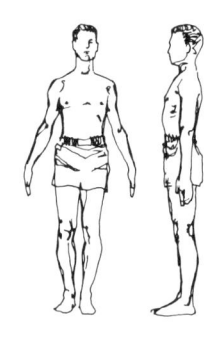

FIGURE 93. *Somatotype 343*

Description: Mid-range Mesomorph. 4th commonest male. One-twentieth of population.

Weight for Age and Height

Height (inches)	18	23	28	33	38	43	48	53	58	63
75	183	190	195	201	205	209	214	215	217	217
74	176	182	188	193	197	201	205	207	208	208
73	169	175	180	185	189	193	197	199	200	200
72	162	168	172	177	181	185	189	190	191	191
71	156	161	166	170	174	178	181	183	184	184
70	150	155	159	163	167	170	174	175	177	177
69	143	148	153	157	160	164	167	168	169	169
68	137	142	146	150	153	157	160	161	162	162
67	131	136	139	143	146	149	152	154	155	155
66	125	129	133	137	140	143	146	147	148	148
65	119	124	127	131	133	136	139	140	141	141
64	114	118	121	125	127	130	133	134	134	134
63	109	113	116	119	121	124	127	128	128	128
62	104	108	110	113	116	118	121	122	122	122
61	99	102	105	108	110	113	115	116	116	116

Atlas of Men, p. 149.

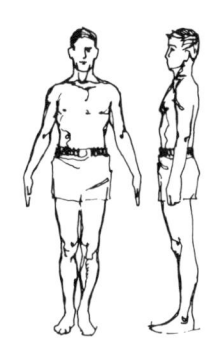

FIGURE 94. *Somatotype 344*

Description: Mesomorph-Ectomorph. Commonest college male. May be longest-lived of all somatotypes.

Weight for Age and Height

Height (inches)	18	23	28	33	38	43	48	53	58	63
75	175	183	188	192	196	200	202	203	204	205
74	168	176	180	185	189	192	194	195	195	197
73	162	169	173	178	181	184	187	187	188	189
72	155	162	166	170	173	176	179	179	180	181
71	148	155	159	163	167	169	172	172	173	174
70	142	149	153	157	160	163	165	165	166	167
69	137	143	147	150	153	156	158	159	159	160
68	131	137	140	144	147	149	151	152	152	153
67	125	131	134	137	140	143	144	145	146	146
66	119	125	128	131	134	136	138	138	139	140
65	114	119	122	125	128	130	132	132	133	133
64	109	114	117	119	122	124	126	126	127	127
63	104	109	111	114	116	118	120	120	121	121
62	99	103	106	109	111	113	114	115	115	116
61	94	99	101	103	105	108	109	109	110	110

Atlas of Men, p. 157.

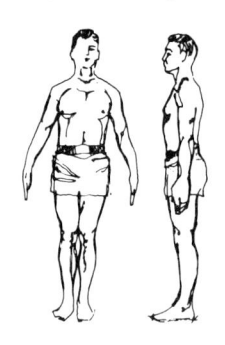

FIGURE 95. *Somatotype 353*

Description: Common Mesomorph. Average athletic type.

Weight for Age and Height

Height (inches)	18	23	28	33	38	43	48	53	58	63
75	191	199	206	214	221	223	227	228	230	230
74	184	191	198	205	212	215	218	219	221	221
73	177	184	190	197	204	207	210	210	212	212
72	169	176	182	189	195	198	201	201	203	202
71	162	169	174	181	187	190	193	193	195	195
70	156	162	167	174	180	182	185	186	187	187
69	149	156	161	167	172	175	177	178	179	179
68	143	149	154	160	165	168	169	170	171	170
67	136	142	147	153	158	160	162	163	164	164
66	130	136	140	146	151	153	155	156	156	156
65	124	130	134	139	144	146	148	149	149	149
64	119	124	128	133	137	139	141	142	142	141
63	113	118	122	127	131	133	134	135	136	136
62	108	113	116	121	124	127	128	129	130	130
61	103	107	111	115	119	121	122	123	123	123

Atlas of Men, p. 169.

Tying It All Together

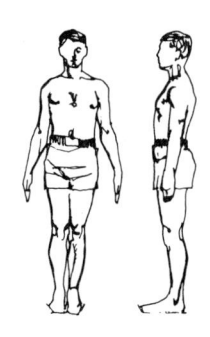

FIGURE 96. *Somatotype 443*

Description: Balanced Endomorph-Mesomorph. Most frequent somatotype. Classic "Common Man."

Weight for Age and Height

Height (inches)	18	23	28	33	38	43	48	53	58	63
75	189	198	209	217	223	231	234	234	234	234
74	181	190	201	208	214	222	224	224	224	224
73	174	183	193	200	206	213	216	216	216	216
72	167	175	185	191	197	204	207	207	207	207
71	160	168	177	184	189	196	198	198	198	198
70	154	162	170	177	182	188	190	190	190	190
69	147	155	163	169	174	180	182	182	183	183
68	141	148	156	162	167	172	174	174	175	175
67	135	142	149	155	159	165	167	167	167	167
66	129	135	142	148	152	157	159	159	160	160
65	123	129	136	141	145	150	152	157	152	152
64	117	123	130	134	138	143	145	145	145	145
63	112	118	124	128	132	137	138	138	139	139
62	106	112	118	122	126	130	132	132	132	132
61	101	107	113	116	120	124	125	125	126	126

Atlas of Men, p. 219.

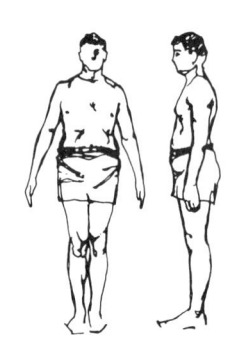

FIGURE 97. *Somatotype 533*

Description: Commonest Endormorph. This is probably the most common female somatotype.

Weight for Age and Height

Height (inches)	18	23	28	33	38	43	48	53	58	63
75	199	210	220	232	244	249	252	250	249	246
74	190	201	210	222	232	238	241	239	238	235
73	183	193	202	213	222	229	232	230	228	226
72	175	185	193	204	213	219	222	220	219	217
71	168	178	186	196	205	211	213	211	210	208
70	162	170	178	188	196	202	205	203	202	200
69	155	164	171	180	188	194	196	193	193	192
68	148	157	164	172	180	185	188	186	185	183
67	142	149	157	165	172	177	179	178	177	175
66	135	143	149	157	165	169	171	169	169	167
65	129	136	143	150	157	161	164	162	161	160
64	123	130	136	143	150	154	156	154	154	153
63	118	124	130	137	143	147	149	147	147	145
62	112	118	124	130	136	140	142	141	140	138
61	107	113	118	124	130	133	135	134	133	132

Atlas of Men, p. 267.

References

1. G. Hooks, *Application of Weight Training to Athletics*, pp. 117-157.
2. *Ibid.*
3. Jean Mayer, "Exercise And Weight Control," *Exercise and Fitness:* A Collection of Papers Presented at the Colloquium on Exercise and Fitness (The University of Illinois: The Athletic Institute, 1959) pp. 110-134.
4. L. J. Bogert, *Nutrition and Physical Fitness*, 7th ed. (Philadelphia: W. B. Saunders, 1961) p. 325.
5. *Ibid.*, p. 327.
6. *Ibid.*, p. 329.
7. J. Mayer, and B. Bullen, "Nutrition and Athletic Performance," *Exercise and Fitness* Colloquium, p. 127.
8. W. Guild, "Pre-Event Nutrition With Some Implications For Endurance Athleties," *Exercise and Fitness* Colloquium, p. 136.
9. J. Mayer, and B. Bullen, *op. cit.*, p. 133.
10. *Ibid.*, p. 124.

Glossary

Adaptation: the attempt by the body to adjust to an overload situation; a change in the level of bodily functioning to keep up with the environmental demands.

Antagonistic muscles: muscles which act to limit the extent of activity of primary contracting muscles.

"Big Four": the four components of physical fitness around which the exercise programs in this book are formed. They are cardiovascular efficiency, strength, local-muscle-endurance, and flexibility.

Cardio-respiratory system: the functional organization of the cardiovascular system and the lungs; the relationships among the various organs responsible for supplying oxygen to and removing carbon dioxide from the various body tissues.

Cardiovascular system: the primary circulatory mechanism of the body; includes the heart, the blood vessels, and the blood.

Circuit Training: a system of general conditioning utilizing stations or areas for exercising. The conditioner moves from station to station, and varies the work load, the repetitions, and the time working from day to day.

Conditioner: a person involved in a conditioning program; one who is exercising.

Conditioning: the process of improving the functionability of the physical aspects of the human organism.

Eccentric contraction: a contraction in which the muscle fibers actively lengthen from a shortened state.

Ectomorph: a somatotype that gives the impression of being thin, bony, and stretched-out; linear skeleton; the last number of the three symbols used in somatotyping.

Efficient movement: skilled motions of body parts in which no extraneous actions or excess energy are present; relative to the purpose of the movement.

Endomorph: a somatotype that gives the impression of obesity; large abdominal area; the first number of the three symbols used in somatotyping.

Flexibility: the property of the body which denotes its range of motion; used mostly to refer to the ability of a muscle to stretch; the range of movement possible to a body part about a joint or series of joints.

Hooke's Law: the physical principle stating that a property stretches in proportion to its ability to return to its original shape; used here in discussion of flexibiliy.

Glossary

Interval Training: a method of cardiovascular conditioning involving the use of alternating work-rest periods; a systematized approach to training in which the conditioner is stressed to a maximum by brief, highly-taxing bouts of exercise. These bouts are increased in difficulty periodically.

Inverse Stretch Reflex: an involuntary motor response to a stretching of the muscle, which produces a lessening of tension within the muscle; to be compared with the Simple Stretch Reflex.

Isometric contraction: a contraction in which the muscle fibers are tensed, but no real shortening in length occurs in them.

Isotonic contraction: a contraction in which the muscle fibers shorten in length.

Kraus-Weber Tests: a series of tests for minimal physical fitness administered originally in the early 1950's on American and European children by Drs. Kraus and Weber.

Local-muscle-endurance: a component of physical functioning; the ability of a muscle to make repeated movements continuously over a period of time; the ability of a muscle to work for a prolonged period of time against a resistance.

Mesomorph: a somatotype that gives the impression of muscularity, firmness; larger thoracic area than abdominal; the second number of the three symbols used in somatotyping.

Muscle coordination: the ability of the muscles to work together to produce a fluid, skilled movement relatively void of wasted motion.

Muscle power: the ability of the muscle to produce movement quickly against a resistance.

Muscle tone: a state of tension within the muscle during non-contracting periods produced either by a fluid concentration or a small nervous stimulation that is rotating among the fibers.

Neutralizing muscles: muscles which act to stabilize the skeleton during a movement.

Overload Principle: the principle which postulates that the organism can only gain in functional capacity by being stressed beyond the work load to which it is accustomed.

Oxygen debt: the physiological term for the amount of oxygen used after exercise above that which ordinarily would be used during rest for the same length of time.

Peripheral circulation: the circultion of blood in the extremities of the body, the legs, the arms, or the head.

Primary muscles: the principal muscles involved in the production of a movement.

Repetitions: the number of times that a particular exercise-movement is executed continuously.

Resistance: anything capable of restricting movement.

Resting pulse: heart beats during period of relative inactivity.

Sets: the number of times during a single workout period that an exercise is performed.

Simple Stretch Reflex: an involuntary motor response to a stretching of the muscle, which produces tension in the muscle; to be compared with the Inverse Stretch Reflex.

Somatotype: a term used to indicate the body type, or morphological design, of an individual.

Strength: a component of physical functioning; the ability to exert force in one maximal effort; the ability of a muscle to exert force against a resistance.

"Trained Person": a person who has conditioned his physical attributes beyond the normal sedentary level; a person whose physical fitness is close to his maximum potential; a person who has undergone an extended period of exercise.

Weight-lifting: exercising with barbells and dumbbells; associated with competition, not necessarily with use in personal conditioning.

Weight-training: exercising with barbells and dumbbells for the purpose of improving strength and local-muscle-endurance.

Bibliography

Bogert, L. J. *Nutrition and Physical Fitness*, 7th ed., Philadelphia: W. B. Saunders, 1961.

Carlsten, A., and G. Grimby. *The Circulatory Response to Muscle Exercise in Man.* Springfield, Ill.: Charles C Thomas, Publisher, 1966.

Cureton, T. K. *Physical Fitness Appraisal and Guidance.* St. Louis, Mo.: The C. V. Mosby Company, 1947.

Daniels, A. S., and E. Davies. *Adapted Physical Education.* New York: Harper & Row, Publishers, 1965.

Davis, E. C., G. A. Logan, and W. C. McKinney. *Biophysical Values of Muscular Activity.* Dubuque, Iowa: Wm. C. Brown Company, 1965.

DeVries, H. A. *Physiology of Exercise.* Dubuque, Iowa: Wm. C. Brown Company, 1966.

Exercise and Fitness: A Collection of Papers Presented at the Colloquium on Exercise and Fitness. Monticello, Illinois: The Athletic Institute, 1959.

Fleishman, E. A. *The Structure and Measurement of Physical Fitness.* Englewood Cliffs, N. J.: Prentice-Hall, Inc., 1964.

Hettinger, T. *Physiology of Strength.* Springfield, Ill.: Charles C Thomas, Publisher, 1961.

Hooks, G. *Application of Weight Training to Athletics.* Englewood Cliffs, N. J.: Prentice-Hall, Inc., 1962.

Karpovich, P. V. *Physiology of Muscular Activity*, 6th ed., Philadelphia: W. B. Saunders, 1965.

Kraus, Hans, and William Raab. *Hypokinetic Disease.* Springfield, Ill.: Charles C Thomas, Publisher, 1961.

Mathews, D. K. *Measurement in Physical Education.* Philadelphia: W. B. Saunders, 1965.

Mathews, D. K., R. W. Stacy, and G. N. Hoover. *Exercise Physiology.* New York: The Ronald Press Company, 1964.

Morehouse, L. E., and A. T. Miller. *Physiology of Exercise.* St. Louis, Mo.: The C. V. Mosby Company, 1959.

Royal Canadian Air Force Exercise Plans For Physical Fitness. New York: Pocket Books, Inc., 1962.

Schifferes, Justus J. *Essentials of Healthier Living.* New York: John Wiley and Sons, Inc., 1963.

Sheldon, W. H. *Atlas Of Men.* New York: Harper & Row, Publishers, 1954.

Sorani, R. P. *Circuit Training.* Dubuque, Iowa: Wm. C. Brown Company, 1966.

Articles

Brouha, L., *et al.* "Studies in Physical Efficiency of College Students," *Research Quarterly*, XV (October, 1944) pp. 211-224.

Clarke, H. H., and D. Glines. "Relationships of Reaction, Movement, and Completion Times to Motor, Strength, Anthropometric, and Maturity Measures of 13-Year-Old Boys," *Research Quarterly*, XXXIII (May, 1962) pp. 194-201.

Cureton, T. K. "Body Build as a Framework of Reference for Interpreting Physical Fitness and Athletic Performance," *Research Quarterly Supplement*, XII (May, 1941) pp. 301-330.

DiGiovanna, V. "The Relation of Selected Structural and Functional Measures to Success in College Athletics," *Research Quarterly*, XIV (May, 1943) pp. 199-216.

Heusner, W. W. "Specificity of Interval Training," East Lansing, Michigan: Michigan State University, 1963, 38 pp.

Sills, F. D., and P. W. Everett. "The Relationship of Extreme Somatotypes to Performance in Motor and Strength Tests," *Research Quarterly*, XXIV (May, 1953) pp. 223-228.

Sills, F. D., and J. Mitchem. "Prediction of Performances on Physical Fitness Tests by Means of Somatotype Ratings," *Research Quarterly*, XXVIII (March, 1957) pp. 64-71.

Index

All or None law, 29
Application of Weight Training to Athletics, 94, 104, 105
Athlete's heart, 106
Atlas, Charles, 59
Atlas of Men, 22, 114

Bogert, L. J., 108, 113

Cardiovascular fitness (*see* Fitness)
Cardiovascular system, 5, 26
Carlston, A., 6
Chamberlain, Wilt, 104
"Cheat curls," 70
Circuit training, 52-56
    5BX Plan, 53-54
    U.S.C. Circuit, 53
    modified (*Table*), 56
Cureton, T., 21

DeVries, H., 28

Eccentric contractions, 58
Ectomorphy, 20-24, 112, 115, 121
Endomorphy, 20-24, 117, 123, 124
Exercise:
    and longevity (*Table*), 1-2
    losing weight, 107-108

Fatigue (*see* muscle fatigue)

Fitness:
    Cardiovascular, 26-27, 46-56
    endurance, 26-27
    reasons for, 1-5
    respiratory, 5-9, 26-27
    tests, 10
Flexibility:
    definition, 9
    exercises, 36-45
    limiting factors, 27-28
    normal range of motion, 10-11
    test, 9, 10
Foster Test, 7-8, 17

Harvard Step Test:
    explanation, 6
    norms, 8
Hooke's Law, 10
Hooks, G., 94, 104, 105

Interval training, 46-52
Isometric contraction:
    definition, 58
    uses, 59, 104, 106
Isotonic contraction, 57
Iowa, University of, 104

Karpovich, P., 6
Kraus, H., 1
Kraus-Weber Tests (*see* Fitness)

Lactic acid (*see* Muscle)

Massage, 110-111
Mathews, D., 6
Mayer, J., 107
Mesomorphy, 20-24, 116, 118, 120, 121, 122, 123
Muscle:
  boundedness, avoiding, 100-101
  co-ordination, 4, 64-66
  fatigue, 29-32
  lactic acid, 31
  levers, 61-62
  local endurance, 12, 29-32, 60-61, 67
  power, 61-63
  reaction to stretching, 28-29
  strength, 12, 32-33, 59-60, 67
  tests for strength and endurance, 12-17
  scores, 18
  tone, 63-64

Obesity, 1, 107-112
  suggested diet, 109
  suggested exercise, 111
Overload Principle, 33-34, 48
Oxygen debt, 49-50

Physical fitness, 1-4
  and appearance, 3-4
  and emotional stability, 3

Pulse rate:
  average for men, 7
  factors affecting, 8-9
  resting, 7

Raab, W., 1
Respiratory fitness (*see*.Fitness)

Sheldon, W., 20-22
Somatotype:
  descriptions, 115-124
  explanation, 20
  Physique Rating Scale, 21
Sorani, R., 52
Strength (*see* muscle strength)
Stretch reflex, 28-29, 65-66
  Inverse, 28-29
  Simple, 28

Valsalva Phenomenon, 101

Warm-up, 35, 38, 60, 103
Weight:
  Charts, 114-124
  "normal," 114
Weight training, 53, 59, 66, 69-101, 104
Williams, Ted, 104

Zatopek, Emil, 47

61103